UNIVERSITY OF NOTRE DAME
WARD-PHILLIPS LECTURES IN
ENGLISH LANGUAGE AND LITERATURE
VOLUME 3

The Wit of Love

Frontispiece. Gerhard Seghers (1591–1651): "St. Teresa in Ecstasy." (*Antwerp: Koninklijk Museum voor Schone Kunsten.*)

The Wit
of
Love

Donne   Carew
Crashaw   Marvell

LOUIS L. MARTZ

THE UNIVERSITY OF NOTRE DAME PRESS
NOTRE DAME   LONDON

Library of Congress Catalog Card Number: 70-85345
Manufactured in the United States of America

To My Sister Lucille

Preface

The essays that follow have been considerably revised and extended since the occasion of their original delivery as lectures in March, 1968. In reworking them I have kept many traces of oral presentation, since these qualities seemed essential to the basic composition of each piece. I am glad to remember them as lectures, since they remind me of the gracious hospitality of the University of Notre Dame, and of the generous, receptive audiences that helped me to understand my own thoughts. I wish to express my gratitude to everyone concerned with the thoughtful arrangements for the Ward-Phillips Lectures during my week at Notre Dame, with many friendly, stimulating conversations and informal gatherings. I am especially grateful to Professor Ernest Sandeen for many favors, including his help in choosing a title for this book; and to Professors Rufus Rauch and Walter Davis for hospitality and for illuminating discussion of many seventeenth-century matters. I am grateful to Miss Emily Schossberger, Director of the University of Notre Dame Press, for her interest in the design of this book, and to Dean Porter, Curator of the University of Notre Dame Art Gallery, for arranging to take photographs of the altarpiece in the University Church.

I owe my thanks to many people for special aspects of this book. Mr. Thomas Wragg, Librarian and Keeper of the Devonshire Collection at Chatsworth, made it possible for me to spend rewarding hours with the Inigo Jones drawings at Chatsworth, and also arranged to send me photographs of certain drawings, along with the permission to reproduce them here. The Courtauld Institute of Art has provided excellent photographs of the Inigo Jones drawings and of the statue of John Donne in St. Paul's. The Very Reverend Martin Sullivan, Dean of St. Paul's, kindly allowed me to view the portrait of Donne that hangs in the Deanery, and has also given his permission to reproduce it here. Mr. D. M. Davin, of the Clarendon Press, has helped me in gaining a photograph of the Deanery portrait of Donne. Miss A. H. Scott-Elliot, Keeper of Prints and Drawings in the Royal Library, Windsor Castle, has generously assisted me in gaining photographs of the miniatures of John Donne and Queen Henrietta Maria. Mrs. Margaret Cousland, of the Lord Chamberlain's Office, has provided me with the photographs of the Van Dyck portraits here reproduced.

The Marquess of Lothian has given his kind permission to reproduce the portrait of Donne in his possession. Miss Caroline Brown, of the National Portrait Gallery, has provided me with a photograph of the Lothian portrait of Donne, along with a photograph of the portrait of Andrew Marvell. Sir Geoffrey Keynes has generously allowed me to examine the Leconfield Manuscript of Donne's poetry in his possession. Mr. A. R. B. Fuller, Librarian of St. Paul's Cathedral Library, has allowed me to examine the St. Paul's Manuscript of Donne's poetry and has helped me to acquire a photograph of the Deanery portrait of Donne. Mr. E. T. Floyd Ewin, Registrar of St. Paul's, has assisted me in gaining a photograph of the statue of Donne, along with permission to reproduce it here. Mr. Herbert F. Potter, Secretary-Treasurer of the Church of All Hallows Barking, has kindly provided me with a photograph of the font-cover ascribed to Grinling Gibbons, along with permission to reproduce it here. Dr. A. Monballieu, of the Koninklijk Museum, Antwerp, has provided me with valuable advice concerning the provenance of the Seghers painting of St. Teresa, and has assisted me in gaining a photograph of this picture, along with permission to reproduce it here. The Fondation Cultura in Brussels has been of great help in providing a photograph of, and information concerning, the version of the Seghers painting that exists in the English Convent at Bruges. I am grateful to the Bodleian Library, the Cambridge University Library, and the British Museum, for allowing me to examine various manuscripts of Donne in their possession. My wife, Edwine Montague, has lent her scholarly assistance in the verification of my manuscript. Mrs. Fannie Gillette has typed and retyped, with scrupulous accuracy, several versions of this book. To all of the above I express my deep appreciation.

Finally, I would like to mention a debt to the exhibition of Van Dyck's paintings presented in the Queen's Gallery, Buckingham Palace, during the summer of 1968. This beautiful exhibition of newly cleaned paintings, along with its excellent catalogue, created a vivid sense of the "Cavalier World" at a time when I was engaged in revising and selecting illustrations for the lectures. This exhibition also contained a number of the finest miniatures of the era, including the Oliver portrait of Donne and, as an item acquired too late for inclusion in the catalogue, the Hoskins miniature of Henrietta Maria, purchased by the Queen in June, 1968. A special notice at the exhibition identified the costume in the miniature as that worn by Henrietta Maria in the production of *Tempe Restord* (see the *Times* [London], May 28, 1968, pp. 12, 14; June 5, 1968, p. 1).

Louis L. Martz

Saybrook College
Yale University
March 25, 1969

Contents

Illustrations

I

John Donne

Love's Philosophy

I

John Donne

Love's Philosophy

One way of grasping the variety of John Donne's career and personality is to ponder the various portraits of Donne that have come down to us from different stages of his life, from the age of eighteen until his death-bed. We have no such variety of portraits for any other poet of this era; and this variety may be taken to indicate some essential qualities of Donne, including his well-known admiration for the art of painting, which led him to fill his house in London with pictures. The last point we know from the touching way in which he distributes various paintings to his friends in his will.

> To Doctor King my executor I give that medal of gold of the synod of Dort which the estates presented me withal at the Hague as also the two pictures of Padre Paolo and Fulgentio which hang in the parlour at my house at Paul's and to Doctor Montford my other executor I give forty ounces of white plate and the two pictures that hang on the same side of the parlour.

Item I give to the right honourable the Earl of Carlisle the picture of the blessed Virgin Mary which hangs in the little dining-chamber. And to the right honourable the Earl of Dorset the picture of Adam and Eve which hangs in the great chamber.

Item I give to Doctor Winniff Dean of Gloucester and residentiary of St. Paul's the picture called the Skeleton which hangs in the Hall and to my kind friend Mr. George Garrard the picture of Mary Magdalene in my chamber and to my ancient friend Doctor Brook, Master of Trinity College in Cambridge the picture of the blessed Virgin and Joseph which hangs in my study and to Mr. Tourvall a French Minister (but by the ordination of the English Church) I give any picture which he will choose of those which hang in the little dining-room and are not formerly bequeathed.

* * * * *

Item I give to my honourable and faithful friend Mr. Robert Carr of his Majesty's bed-chamber that picture of mine which is taken in shadows and was made very many years before I was of this profession. And to my honourable friend Sir John Danvers I give what picture he shall accept of those that remain unbequeathed.[1]

The earliest of the portraits of Donne that have come down to us is the one that appears as the frontispiece for the 1635 edition of his poetry, a portrait based, it seems, upon a lost original by Nicholas Hilliard. It is dated in 1591 at the age of eighteen, and it shows the picture of a young cavalier, with long curled locks, a large earring, and a sword firmly grasped by the hilt. Above is a motto in Spanish which reads in translation "Sooner dead than changed," a motto taken from a song in a popular pastoral romance, the *Diana* of Montemayor.

ANNO DNI. 1591.
ÆTATIS SVÆ 18

ANTES MVDADO
MVERTO QVE

This was for youth, Strength, Mirth, and wit that Time
Most count their golden Age; but t'was not thine.
Thine was thy later yeares, so much refind
From youths Drosse, Mirth, & wit; as thy pure mind
Thought (like the Angels) nothing but the Praise
Of thy Creator, in those last, best Dayes.
   Witnes this Booke, (thy Embleme) which begins
   With Love; but endes, with Sighes, & Teares for sins.

Will: Marshall. sculpsit.   IZ:WA:

Figure 1. John Donne at the age of 18. Frontispiece to the
second edition of Donne's *Poems*, 1635.

Figure 2. John Donne: the Lothian Portrait.
(*Reproduced by kind permission of the Marquess of Lothian.*)

TWENTY-TWO

The next portrait is the one referred to in Donne's will as "that picture of mine which is taken in shadows"; it was rediscovered by John Bryson ten years ago in the possession of the Marquess of Lothian.[2] This is an even more striking picture, presenting Donne in the costume and the manner of a melancholy lover,[3] with a large dark hat, a fine lace collar, carelessly thrown open at the neck, thin tapering fingers, and in the background the motto "Illumina tenebr[as] nostras Domina" ("Enlighten our darkness, Lady"). This is a witty adaptation of a prayer from the service of Compline in the Sarum *Breviarium*: "Illumina quesumus domine deus tenebras nostras"—words that have passed into the *Book of Common Prayer* for the service of Evensong: "Lighten our darkness, we beseech thee, O Lord."[4]

The next is a superb miniature now in the Library of Windsor Castle, signed with the monogram of Isaac Oliver, and dated 1616, when Donne was about forty-four years old:

Figure 3. John Donne at the age of 44. Miniature by Isaac Oliver, 1616. (*Royal Library, Windsor Castle; reproduced by gracious permission of Her Majesty Queen Elizabeth II.*)

a year after he had entered the priesthood of the English Church. It presents Donne in the mode of a newly ordained preacher, with pointed beard, high collar of pleated ruff, deep circles under the eyes, and a sober, almost ascetic expression.

Fourthly, there is a portrait that hangs in the Deanery at St. Paul's, inscribed *"Aetatis Suae* 49 1620"—the year before Donne was made the Dean of St. Paul's. He is dressed here in what looks like a scholar's lounging-robe; the expression shows the beginning of a pleasant smile, with an effect of ease and happiness that we do not often associate with Donne. The whole figure presents an image of secure achievement and profound wisdom, an impression reinforced by the fact that the painting is conceived in that favorite form of the High Renaissance, the circular or *tondo* form.

Finally, we have that strange and wonderful effigy carved in marble and still visible in St. Paul's, said to be the only piece of the Cathedral's statuary saved from the great fire of 1666. The occasion of the statue is described by Izaak Walton in his *Life of Donne*, where he tells us that a few weeks before Donne's death, in the full knowledge that he was dying, Donne was persuaded by his physician to have a monument made of himself, and this Donne proceeded to do in the following fashion:

> A Monument being resolved upon, Dr. *Donne* sent for a Carver to make for him in wood the figure of an *Urn*, giving him directions for the compass and height of it; and to bring with it a board of the just height of his body. These being got: then without delay a choice Painter was got to be in a readiness to draw his Picture, which was taken as followeth.— Several Charcole-fires being first made in his large Study, he

Figure 4. John Donne at the age of 49. (*The Deanery of St. Paul's Cathedral; reproduced by kind permission of the Very Reverend the Dean of St. Paul's. Photo: Fleming.*)

brought with him into that place his winding-sheet in his hand, and, having put off all his cloaths, had this sheet put on him, and so tyed with knots at his head and feet, and his hands so placed, as dead bodies are usually fitted to be shrowded and put into their Coffin, or grave. Upon this *Urn* he thus stood with his eyes shut, and with so much of the sheet turned aside as might shew his lean, pale, and death-like face, which was purposely turned toward the East, from whence he expected the second coming of his and our Saviour Jesus.' In this posture he was drawn at his just height; and when the Picture was fully finished, he caused it to be set by his bed-side, where it continued, and became his hourly object till his death: and, was then given to his dearest friend and Executor Doctor *Henry King*, . . . who caused him to be thus carved in one entire piece of white Marble, as it now stands in that Church . . .[5]

I mention all these portraits to suggest, first of all, Donne's lifelong practice of adopting dramatic postures, in many different attitudes, his way of constantly creating fictional roles out of aspects of his personality. As in his portraits, so in his poetry the complex personality that we call "Donne" is created by means of a continually shifting series of dramatic moments, spoken in a voice that we recognize, even while the voice presents an astonishing variety of roles. Whether Donne appears as the cavalier, the lover, the priest, the scholar, or the dying man, all of these were part of John Donne's awareness of himself at all stages of his career,[6] some aspects emerging into dominance while other aspects remained recessive for a time, to emerge as dominant at other times—sometimes, it almost seems, on the next day, or in the next hour.

Donne's own deep knowledge of himself, gained by relent-

Figure 5. John Donne in his shroud. Marble statue by Nicholas Stone, c. 1631. (*St. Paul's Cathedral; reproduced by kind permission of the Dean and Chapter of St. Paul's.*)

Figure 6. John Donne in his shroud. Frontispiece to Donne's last sermon, *Deaths Duell*, published 1632. Engraved either from the statue by Stone or perhaps from the painting made as a design for this statue.

less self-scrutiny, is revealed by the analysis of his varied moods that he gives in that famous sonnet, so personal and private that it exists in only one manuscript and remained unpublished until the year 1899:

> Oh, to vex me, contraryes meete in one:
> Inconstancy unnaturally hath begott
> A constant habit; that when I would not
> I change in vowes, and in devotione.
> As humorous is my contritione
> As my prophane love, and as soone forgott:

—"humorous," that is, capricious, changeable, unsteady; "ridlingly distemperd," as he goes on to say, that is, disordered, in a state of puzzling instability:

> As ridlingly distemperd, cold and hott,
> As praying, as mute; as infinite, as none.
> I durst not view heaven yesterday; and to day
> In prayers, and flattering speaches I court God:
> To morrow I quake with true feare of his rod.
> So my devout fitts come and go away
> Like a fantastique Ague: save that here
> Those are my best dayes, when I shake with feare.[7]

Here, in his religious mood, Donne says, those are his best days when he shakes with the fear of God, but as a worldly lover his worst days were those when he feared his Lady did not love him.

What we see in this sonnet, as in the whole great series of portraits, is the image of a man who is attempting to hold within his consciousness an almost unbearable range of interests. In fact, Donne, both in his life and in his literary works, represents every aspect of the European Renaissance. His first portrait is that of a military man, and indeed, he sailed with the Earl of Essex on two arduous military voyages, for a complex of reasons that he himself sums up in his poem "The Calme":

> Whether a rotten state, and hope of gaine,
> Or to disuse mee from the queasie paine
> Of being belov'd, and loving, or the thirst
> Of honour, or faire death, out pusht mee first . . .

The reference to his love affairs speaks for itself, while his rash and secret marriage to the sixteen-year-old girl shows the passionate and impulsive nature of his affections. Meanwhile he had been preparing himself by the study of Law for a political career, and indeed, he appears to have served in Parliament. At the depth of his misfortunes he appears even to have considered emigrating to Virginia. At the same time his famous reference to his "hydroptique immoderate desire of humane learning and languages"[8] shows his full participation in the Renaissance love of letters. He travelled in France, Italy and Spain, and had some command of the languages of those three countries, along with his powerful command of Latin. The high quality of the portraits that he commissioned and the number of paintings contained in his house (including, it seems, a Madonna by Titian)[9] show his deep participation in the visual arts. And finally, more than any other writer of his time, Donne lived at the intense center of controversy between the Catholic and the Protestant currents of religion. Bred as a Roman Catholic in a family noted for its sufferings under persecution, Donne studied the whole body of "controverted divinity," and ultimately became a priest and famous preacher in the Church of England. In this variety of his concerns, then, Donne stands forth as symbolizing all the rich and warring interests of the Renaissance man. And it is these interests that cause the anguish and the glory of his poetry, for in his poetry the skeptic and the believer exist side by side, the lover of women and the lover of God are not separable, suicidal despair and transcendent faith are racking the speaker in opposite directions at the same time, ambition and asceticism are struggling for dominion in the same hour.

Thus, at the time when Donne was writing his indecent and outrageous love-elegies (those poems where the world of Ovid is pillaged and transformed into a much more ruthless and raging world of passion than the bland and sophisticated Ovid could ever represent), in those years when Donne was a young law student, and just before he departed (in 1596 and 1597) to participate in those two military voyages, just then in his famous Satire III Donne is found denouncing all these ventures, and demanding that his soul and ours must seek true religion: "O where?" Others, he says, speaking in a double voice both to himself and to his listeners—others may accept religion on easy terms:

> but unmoved thou
> Of force must one, and forc'd but one allow;
> And the right;

"Of force" because it is in his nature to demand one answer; he moves under an inner compulsion, "unmoved" by outward considerations and persuasions. And if "forc'd" in another sense by those who attempt to draw him from the right by threats of persecution or by loss of worldly power, he must still pursue "but one" and "the right."

> To'adore, or scorne an image, or protest,
> May all be bad; doubt wisely; in strange way
> To stand inquiring right, is not to stray;
> To sleepe, or runne wrong, is. On a huge hill,
> Cragged, and steep, Truth stands, and hee that will
> Reach her, about must, and about must goe;
> And what th'hills suddennes resists, winne so;

In this famous passage, indispensable to an understanding of Donne, one feels the strain of thought bending the lines out of the couplet form, as though the rhymes were obstacles to overcome. The whole of the Renaissance, the Reformation, and the Counter-Reformation are pressing in upon that poem, demanding one answer to their manifold problems. That God exists, that Truth exists, Donne never doubts; but where these absolutes are to be found on earth, Donne does not know.

This traditional image of the soul's journey up the mountain of Truth, beautifully illustrated in a Florentine painting of the early Renaissance, represents perfectly the agonized effort of Donne's mind to rise above the world of flux represented, from beginning to end, in his poetry—that world of change, corruption, decay, self-seeking, betrayal, disease, and death, which forms the somber ground from which his questing mind seeks to arise. As explained by Roberto Weiss,[10] the hill of Knowledge in this Florentine miniature shows in all its "cragged" or "ragged"[11] stages the process upward from

Figure 7 (opposite). "Turris Sapientiae." Florentine, 15th century (?). (*Chantilly, Musée Condé. Photo: Giraudon.*)

grammar to theology. The aspirant toward Truth is met at the Renaissance doorway by the allegorical figure of Grammar (with the Roman grammarian Donatus writing in the foreground). Beyond the archway sits Pythagoras, the founder of Arithmetic, represented allegorically by the young lady behind him. As we move upward, each female figure, representing one of the seven liberal arts, has seated beneath her the figure of some ancient sage. Thus, we move in the following order: Zeno, with the figure of Logic above him; Tubal Cain, perhaps here fused with Jubal, "Father of all such as handle the harp and organ" (Genesis 4:21), with the figure of Music above him; on the same level the astronomer Ptolemy, with the figure of Astronomy above, holding in her hand an image of the universe; to the left of her the sage Euclid with Geometry above him. Next comes Cicero, with the figure of Rhetoric above. Then, second from the top, appropriately seated in the center, comes the figure of St. Augustine, who christianized the liberal arts and moved them upward toward Theology, who sits at the top with one hand holding the symbol of the Trinity, and the other hand pointing upward to the figure of God. I have explained the image in detail, because it shows so well how Donne's quest for Truth included this whole immense inheritance from the Middle Ages and moved it onward through the portal of the Renaissance into a new aesthetic dimension.

That new dimension I should like to explore within the body of Donne's "Songs and Sonets," where Donne's winding quest toward Truth is displayed in the unstable, constantly shifting movement that one feels within many of the best poems, and also in the oscillation that we feel as we move from poem to poem in their traditional order—or disorder.

Donne's love-poems take for their basic theme the problem of the place of human love in a physical world dominated by change and death. The problem is broached in dozens of different ways, sometimes implicitly, sometimes explicitly, sometimes by asserting the immortality of love, sometimes by declaring the futility of love. Thus the "Songs and Sonets" hold within themselves every conceivable attitude toward love threatened by change. At the one extreme lie the cynical, cavalier songs, the famous "Goe, and catche a falling starre," or "The Indifferent," spoken by one who can "love any, so she be not true." Even beyond this, we have the extreme of bitter disillusionment in that somber poem "Farewell to Love," where the poet asks whether love is no more than a gingerbread King discarded after a fair:

> But, from late faire
> His highnesse sitting in a golden Chaire,
>   Is not lesse cared for after three dayes
> By children, then the thing which lovers so
> Blindly admire, and with such worship wooe;
>   Being had, enjoying it decayes:
>   And thence,
> What before pleas'd them all, takes but one sense,
> And that so lamely, as it leaves behinde
> A kinde of sorrowing dulnesse to the minde.

At the other extreme, perhaps only a poem or two after some poem of cynicism, we will find such a poem as "The Undertaking," where Donne moves to the opposite extreme of pure platonic love, challenging the reader with these words:

> But he who lovelinesse within
>   Hath found, all outward loathes,
> For he who colour loves, and skinne,
>   Loves but their oldest clothes.
>
> If, as I have, you also doe
>   Vertue'attir'd in woman see,
> And dare love that, and say so too,
>   And forget the Hee and Shee;
>
> And if this love, though placed so,
>   From prophane men you hide,
> Which will no faith on this bestow,
>   Or, if they doe, deride:
>
> Then you'have done a braver thing
>   Then all the *Worthies* did,
> And a braver thence will spring,
>   Which is, to keepe that hid.

It is clear that the libertine poems are the obverse, the counterpart, the necessary context, for the poems on constancy. The libertine poems express the fatigue, the cynicism, the flippancy, and the bitterness of the disappointed seeker after the One and True, as Donne very clearly says in his poem "Loves Alchymie," which appropriately comes quite precisely in the middle of the "Songs and Sonets," just after the great poem of true love "A Valediction: of Weeping":

> Some that have deeper digg'd loves Myne then I,
> Say, where his centrique happiness doth lie:
>   I have lov'd, and got, and told,

("told" in the sense of "have counted up the results")

But should I love, get, tell, till I were old,
I should not finde that hidden mysterie;
    Oh, 'tis imposture all:

Clearly the "centrique happiness" that is here renounced represents an abstraction that lies beyond the physical. Such a poem
as this represents a violent revulsion against the lover who has
in such a poem as "Aire and Angels" sought for an ideal
beauty and loved an ideal beauty in his imagination:

Twice or thrice had I lov'd thee,
    Before I knew thy face or name;
So in a voice, so in a shapelesse flame,
Angells affect us oft, and worship'd bee;
    Still when, to where thou wert, I came,
Some lovely glorious nothing I did see.
    But since my soule, whose child love is,
Takes limmes of flesh, and else could nothing doe,
    More subtile then the parent is,
Love must not be, but take a body too,
    And therefore what thou wert, and who,
        I bid Love aske, and now
That it assume thy body, I allow,
And fixe it selfe in thy lip, eye, and brow.

But he discovers that her physical beauty is too dazzling for
love to work upon and that some other abode for his love
must be sought, and so he concludes, referring to the medieval
doctrine that angels appeared to men in forms of mist or
vapor:

Then as an Angell, face, and wings
Of aire, not pure as it, yet pure doth weare,
    So thy love may be my loves spheare;

> Just such disparitie
> As is twixt Aire and Angells puritie,
> 'Twixt womens love, and mens will ever bee.

It may seem at first that the last two lines, with this emphasis upon the superior "purity" of men's love to women's love, are not exactly complimentary to a being of such angelic nature; and yet, when we think of it closely, it is in fact a version of an old Petrarchan compliment. What he is saying is this: if she will extend her love toward him, if she will come down from her angelic status and deign to love a man, then his love for her may move like a planet within her love for him. But why is her love for him less pure than his love for her? Is it not because of the *direction* of their two loves: hers downward toward him, and his upward toward a creature of angelic purity? Donne appears to be combining here the Platonizing love philosophy of the Renaissance[12] with an older tradition, the tradition of the courtly lover inherited by Petrarch, in which the lady is a superior being of angelic purity and beauty, as is the lady of Spenser's sonnets. Donne is here, surprisingly enough, standing by the old Petrarchan tradition in his own winding way.

So it is with Donne's pursuit of love. It has many temporary conclusions, some cynical, some ennobling, but all only "for a moment final," as Wallace Stevens might say. Behind all these varied posturings lies the overwhelming question: what is the nature of love, what is the ultimate ground of love's being? His best poems are not those which move toward either extreme in his answer, but they are rather those in which the physical and the spiritual are made to work together, through the curiously shifting and winding manner that marks Donne's movements toward Truth. One can sense that movement at its best in the poem known as "Loves Growth" (though entitled "Spring" in many of the manuscripts). It opens with the characteristic brooding over the problem of change:

> I scarce beleeve my love to be so pure
>> As I had thought it was,
>> Because it doth endure
> Vicissitude, and season, as the grasse;

With such an opening one might expect that the lover is about to lament the fact that his love has decayed; but, on the contrary, what worries him, what proves the instability of his love, is the fact that it seems to be increasing:

> Me thinkes I lyed all winter, when I swore,
> My love was infinite, if spring make'it more.

What then is the nature of love, he asks?

> But if this medicine, love, which cures all sorrow
>> With more, not onely bee no quintessence,
>> But mixt of all stuffes, paining soule, or sense,
> And of the Sunne his working vigour borrow,
> Love's not so pure, and abstract, as they use
> To say, which have no Mistresse but their Muse,
> But as all else, being elemented too,
> Love sometimes would contemplate, sometimes do.

Having decided then that the nature of love involves the total physical and spiritual being of man, Donne seems to drop the problem entirely in the second half of the poem, shifts his stance completely, and decides that in fact the problem of vicissitude and season does not really exist for this particular love of his:

> And yet not greater, but more eminent,
>   Love by the spring is growne;
>   As, in the firmament,
> Starres by the Sunne are not inlarg'd, but showne.

The scientific sound of the image has a satisfying effect, until one tries to decide exactly what it means, and then, as so often with Donne's conceits, the apparent assurance becomes considerably less sure. "Eminent" is certainly used in the sense of "prominent" but from here on the best commentators disagree. Grierson interprets the lines as meaning "The stars at sunrise are not really made larger, but they are made to seem larger." Miss Gardner, however, takes "by the Sunne" to mean "near the sun," thus: "Love has risen higher in the heavens by spring and shines the more brilliantly as do stars when near to the sun."[13] The latter meaning is almost certainly right, since Donne is not talking about sunrise, but about the rising of the spring. But we are not to examine the image closely; we are simply to gain its positive effect of security in love, as the remaining images continue to assure us with their varied action:

> Gentle love deeds, as blossomes on a bough,
> From loves awaken'd root do bud out now.
> If, as in water stir'd more circles bee
>   Produc'd by one, love such additions take,
>   Those like so many spheares, but one heaven make,
> For, they are all concentrique unto thee;

> And though each spring doe adde to love new heate,
> As princes doe in times of action get
> New taxes, and remit them not in peace,
> No winter shall abate the springs encrease.

But the last word "encrease" would appear to contradict the beginning of this stanza. If there has been "encrease" then love must have grown greater and love must not then be so pure as he had thought it was. And indeed, if we look closely at the last stanza we see that it does not basically deal with the assurance affirmed in the first four lines of that stanza, but rather carries on from the last line of the first stanza, "Love sometimes would contemplate, sometimes do." It soon appears that the speaker is talking about "love-deeds" and that it is love in action that he wishes to see develop: these are the additions that love will take, like circlès stirred in water, or like "spheares" about one center. New heat is not a quality of a pure substance, in the scientific sense that Donne is broaching in the poem's first line. Love deeds, the buds of spring, circles in the water, the new heat of the season—all these are part of a transient and fluctuating physical universe. And indeed the surprising image

> As princes doe in times of action get
> New taxes, and remit them not in peace,

brings us vividly into the realistic world. Thus the assertion at the end, "No winter shall abate the springs encrease" stands as a defiance against all the imagery of vicissitude that dominates the poem. We may believe the assertion, or we may believe the whole poem. In the end, I think, the poem is bound to win.

One can never be sure, then, where Donne's probing of the problem of mutability will lead. This is especially clear in the two poems where Donne uses, in different ways, his image "A bracelet of bright haire about the bone." In "The Funerall" the poem begins by creating a symbol of constancy and immortality out of the "wreath of haire," as the speaker imagines himself dead:

> Who ever comes to shroud me, do not harme
>> Nor question much
> That subtile wreath of haire, which crowns mine arme;
> The mystery, the signe you must not touch,
>> For 'tis my outward Soule,
> Viceroy to that, which then to heaven being gone,
>> Will leave this to controule,
> And keepe these limbes, her Provinces, from dissolution.

But, as with many of Donne's most resounding affirmations, the more the speaker broods about this and attempts to prove its truth, the more it tends to disintegrate. Here, in paralleling the mistress's hair with the nerves that run throughout his body, he is led toward a glimpse of his Lady herself:

> These haires which upward grew, and strength and art
> Have from a better braine . . .

This memory of the Lady in her actual life suggests to him another and more cruel possibility in keeping with her nature:

> Except she meant that I
> By this should know my pain,
> As prisoners then are manacled, when they'are condemn'd
> to die.

He does not know what she could mean by such a gift and in despair he swaggers with his "bravery," uttering at the end what amounts to a rude innuendo:

> What ere shee meant by'it, bury it with me,
>   For since I am
> Loves martyr, it might breed idolatrie,
> If into others hands these Reliques came;
>   As 'twas humility
> To'afford to it all that a Soule can doe,
>   So, 'tis some bravery,
> That since you would save none of mee, I bury some of
>   you.

In "The Relique" the direction of thought is reversed. Whereas "The Funerall" had moved from thoughts of fidelity to cynicism, "The Relique" moves from cynical thoughts about love to an affirmation of a miraculous purity in human love. Thus the poem opens with some of Donne's most satirical innuendoes:

> When my grave is broke up againe
> Some second ghest to entertaine,
> (For graves have learn'd that woman-head
> To be to more then one a Bed)
>   And he that digs it, spies
> A bracelet of bright haire about the bone,
>   Will he not let'us alone,
> And thinke that there a loving couple lies,
> Who thought that this device might be some way
> To make their soules, at the last busie day,
> Meet at this grave, and make a little stay?

THE WIT OF LOVE

Donne accepts the fact that even graves are not sacred, and
suggests in the last few lines above that perhaps someone
would think that this erotic symbol would indicate that some
"loving couple" have arranged for a last carnal assignation
even while the Judge is busy with his work of salvation and
damnation. But, as it turns out, this is not at all what these
two lovers had in mind. She is not a Mary Magdalene, that is
to say, a reformed prostitute, and he is nothing of the kind
either. It is only the continuous misunderstanding of man,
whether in the field of religion or in the field of love, that
makes it certain that people will misinterpret the nature of
this symbol.

> If this fall in a time, or land,
> Where mis-devotion doth command,
> Then, he that digges us up, will bring
> Us, to the Bishop, and the King,
> To make us Reliques; then
> Thou shalt be'a Mary Magdalen, and I
> A something else thereby;
> All women shall adore us, and some men;
> And since at such times, miracles are sought,
> I would that age were by this paper taught
> What miracles wee harmlesse lovers wrought.

> First, we lov'd well and faithfully,
> Yet knew not what wee lov'd, nor why,
> Difference of sex no more wee knew,
> Then our Guardian Angells doe;
> Comming and going, wee
> Perchance might kisse, but not between those meales;
> Our hands ne'r toucht the seales,
> Which nature, injur'd by late law, sets free:

> These miracles wee did; but now alas,
> All measure, and all language, I should passe,
> Should I tell what a miracle shee was.

It is, no doubt, a pure love, as the speaker declares. And yet there is something in the last six lines which doth protest too much. Why should he regard their rare kisses as "meales"? Why should he regard the seals of chastity as a restriction placed upon nature by "late law" which thus injures the freedom of nature itself? And why should, at the end, his feelings falter ("alas") into such a desperate compliment? Perhaps the symbol of eroticism is not so wide of the mark as the speaker declares. In both poems the meaning of that macabre symbol appears to be essentially the same: it suggests the agonized reluctance of Donne to allow any severance between the physical and the spiritual.

In a more obvious way, this reluctance to sever physical and spiritual is shown in the short poem entitled "The Anniversarie," which opens with Donne's most splendid affirmation of the immortality of true love:

> All Kings, and all their favorites,
> All glory'of honors, beauties, wits,
> The Sun it selfe, which makes times, as they passe,
> Is elder by a yeare, now, then it was
> When thou and I first one another saw:
> All other things, to their destruction draw,
>   Only our love hath no decay;
> This, no to morrow hath, nor yesterday,
> Running it never runs from us away,
> But truly keepes his first, last, everlasting day.

The plurality of the word *times* sums up the evanescence of worldly glories, and stresses, by contrast with the great doxology of the last line, the eternity of this true love. But then in the second stanza he remembers that in fact they must part, in some measure:

> Two graves must hide thine and my coarse,
>   If one might, death were no divorce.
> Alas, as well as other Princes, wee,
> (Who Prince enough in one another bee,)
> Must leave at last in death, these eyes, and eares,
> Oft fed with true oathes, and with sweet salt teares;
>   But soules where nothing dwells but love
> (All other thoughts being inmates) then shall prove
> This, or a love increased there above,
> When bodies to their graves, soules from their graves
>   remove.

We feel the strong clinging to the physical; but of course it is a consolation to remember that the souls will be united in heaven—and yet another thought comes upon the speaker as he remembers that in heaven they will lose the unique, distinctive nature of their love because there everyone will be thoroughly blessed—"but wee no more, then all the rest." His mind turns back to earth where their monarchy is unique:

> Here upon earth, we'are Kings, and none but wee
> Can be such Kings, nor of such subjects bee;
> Who is so safe as wee? where none can doe
> Treason to us, except one of us two.
>   True and false feares let us refraine,
> Let us love nobly', and live, and adde againe

> Yeares and yeares unto yeares, till we attaine
> To write threescore: this is the second of our raigne.

We notice how in the last four lines the poet tacitly concedes that this perfect love is not immortal, but is subject to the rule of times. They will celebrate the beginning of the second year of their reign, which will last until they are threescore. He speaks of holding back "True and false feares." The false fear is fear that they will ever be untrue to one another, but the true fear is that their mortal love is indeed subject to mortality.

The same problem gives its deep poignancy to the famous "Valediction: forbidding Mourning," where the affirmation of a spiritual love, presumably between man and wife,[14] has the effect of emphasizing the anguish of being forced to a temporary physical separation. Everyone has admired the delicate opening of the poem in which the separation of lovers is represented as a kind of death-bed scene:

> As virtuous men passe mildly' away,
>   And whisper to their soules, to goe,
> Whilst some of their sad friends doe say,
>   The breath goes now, and some say, no:
>
> So let us melt, and make no noise,
>   No teare-floods, nor sigh-tempests move,
> 'Twere prophanation of our joyes
>   To tell the layetie our love.

What Donne is representing here is the essence of many an airport, or station, or dock-side scene, where true lovers may attempt to repress their tears, not wishing to show the laity their love. And then the poem goes on to say

> Dull sublunary lovers love
>   (Whose soule is sense) cannot admit
> Absense, because it doth remove
>   Those things which elemented it.
> But we by' a love, so much refin'd,
>   That our selves know not what it is,
> Inter-assured of the mind,
>   Care lesse, eyes, lips, and hands to misse.

"Care lesse," but is it so? The very rigor and intricacy of the famous image of the compass at the end may be taken to suggest a rather desperate dialectical effort to control by logic and reason a situation almost beyond rational control.

The whole problem of the relationship between the soul and body in love is brought to a crisis of ambiguity in the frequently-discussed poem, "The Exstasie." This contains a curious and enigmatic combination of traditions in Renaissance poetry and thought. First of all, it grows from the poetical tradition represented by Sidney's Eighth Song in *Astrophil and Stella*,[15] a song in which the lover attempts to persuade the lady in a pastoral setting to give way to the lover's wishes. Donne's prologue in his poem is exactly the same length as Sidney's prologue: seven quatrains. But Donne's interest in nature is so little that it appears as though the flower-bed consists of just a single violet: Donne is not interested in pastoral but in other implications.

> Where, like a pillow on a bed,
>   A Pregnant banke swel'd up, to rest

> The violets reclining head,
> Sat we two, one anothers best;
>
> Our hands were firmely cimented
> With a fast balme, which thence did spring,
> Our eye-beames twisted, and did thred
> Our eyes, upon one double string;
>
> So to'entergraft our hands, as yet
> Was all our meanes to make us one,
> And pictures on our eyes to get
> Was all our propagation.

The physical suggestions of the poem here have led some readers to feel that the following philosophical discourse is simply a smoke-screen, as in "The Flea," for a libertine design. On the other hand, a very strong tradition in Renaissance thought that lies behind the discussion in the rest of the poem has suggested to other readers that it really does present a true debate over love's philosophy.[16] From this standpoint the poem may be seen as an assertion of the purity of human love in all its aspects. The title then is quite ironical. We are not going to witness here an ecstasy of physical passion (as in Carew's "A Rapture"). On the other hand, although we do hear the souls of the lovers speak in a Neoplatonic state of ecstasis, in which the souls go forth from the body to discover the True and the One—nevertheless the Truth that they discover is in fact the Truth of Aristotle and the synthesis of St. Thomas Aquinas: that the soul must work through the body; such is the natural state of man. The last lines prove the purity of their love. If there is small change when the souls are to bodies gone, then spiritual love has succeeded in controlling passion. From this standpoint Donne is misleading us with false expectations by the physical imagery of the opening part. These lovers will probably go off and get properly married in good Spenserian fashion. And indeed the deep self-control of these lovers is perhaps implied by the strictness of the three-part structure that the poem displays, being (more precisely than usual with Donne) divided into setting, analysis, and resolution. The total effect of the poem suggests a philosophical mode of rational control superimposed upon a libertine situation. The libertine suggestions are finally dominated and transcended by a richer, more inclusive, more spiritual view of love.

And yet each poem within the "Songs and Sonets" can be no more than a temporary house of harmony, where Creative Mind, in Yeats's phrase, brings peace out of rage and creates the lovers' stasis and order, for a moment only. Thus, in the traditional order, the affirmation of the perfect "patterne" of love in "The Canonization" is followed at once by the semi-recantation, "The Triple Foole."

> I am two fooles, I know,
> For loving, and for saying so
> In whining Poëtry;
> But where's that wiseman, that would not be I,
> If she would not deny?

And then this half-despairing, half-cynical poem is followed at once by the slow, sad, quiet measures of the beautiful poem entitled "Loves [or "Lovers"] Infiniteness" where the word "all" rings throughout as the dirge of an unattainable Ideal:

> If yet I have not all thy love,
> Deare, I shall never have it all;

> I cannot breath one other sigh, to move,
> Nor can intreat one other teare to fall.
> All my treasure, which should purchase thee,
> Sighs, teares, and oathes, and letters I have spent,
> Yet no more can be due to mee,
> Then at the bargaine made was ment.
> If then thy gift of love were partiall,
> That some to mee, some should to others fall,
> Deare, I shall never have Thee All.

In the fifth line above we should note the excellent reading of Miss Gardner's text, taken from the manuscripts: "All my treasure," in place of the weaker traditional reading "And all my treasure"; for this manuscript reading throws a proper emphasis upon the thematic word "all," binding it with the last word of the stanza and with the end rhymes that reinforce the dirge-like repetitions. But then, in Donne's characteristically winding way, the poem shifts its posture and runs over the same ground from a different point of view, pondering a new possibility which at the close is discarded for yet another point of view:

> Or if then thou gav'st mee all,
> All was but All, which thou hadst then,
> But if in thy heart, since, there be or shall,
> New love created bee, by other men,
> Which have their stocks intire, and can in teares,
> In sighs, in oathes, and letters outbid mee,
> This new love may beget new feares,
> For, this love was not vowed by thee.
> And yet it was, thy gift being generall,
> The ground, thy heart is mine, what ever shall
> Grow there, deare, I should have it all.

But as the third and final stanza opens we find the speaker discarding all these previous possibilities and turning toward a point of view which reaches a temporary conclusion in the powerful echo of one of the most famous of religious paradoxes (Mark 8:35):

> Yet I would not have all yet,
>   Hee that hath all can have no more,
> And since my love doth every day admit
>   New growth, thou shouldst have new rewards in store;
> Thou canst not every day give me thy heart,
>   If thou canst give it, then thou never gav'st it:
> Loves riddles are, that though thy heart depart,
>   It stayes at home, and thou with losing sav'st it:

But these lovers move beyond the Gospel paradox and have, this lover hopes, an even richer future:

> But wee will have a way more liberall,
> Then changing hearts, to joyne them, so wee shall
>   Be one, and one anothers All.

Despite that splendid final affirmation of Oneness, the whole poem creates, through its shifts and oscillations, a sense of the painful unlikelihood that this All will ever really be found. This great poem represents in itself the effect that one feels throughout the "Songs and Sonets"—the poignant fragility of human love. It is the state of lovers summed up for us in "A Lecture upon the Shadow." Here the lover and his Lady have been walking about in the morning, for three hours, in a situation representing the restless, yearning state of lovers seeking what T. S. Eliot calls the "still moment, repose of noon." Now the moment of declaration has come, the moment of "brave clearenesse"—"brave" in the old Elizabethan sense of "splendid," "superb," as well as "brave" in our modern sense. They must now declare their loves and try to maintain them against the world of time. Appropriately, the poem opens by creating the impression that the speaker is attempting, by a deliberate act of will, to force a pause in the flow of time.

> Stand still, and I will read to thee
> A Lecture, Love, in loves philosophy.
>   These three houres that we have spent,
>   Walking here, two shadowes went
> Along with us, which we our selves produc'd;
> But, now the Sunne is just above our head,
>   We doe those shadowes tread;
> And to brave clearenesse all things are reduc'd.
>   So whilst our infant loves did grow,
>   Disguises did, and shadowes, flow
> From us, and our care; but, now 'tis not so.
>
> That love hath not attain'd the high'st degree,
> Which is still diligent lest others see.

Up to this point in time the lovers have been disguising the growth of their love from other people: thus their love has been accompanied by shadows in two senses, by disguises and by the worries that come from fear of revealing their love to other people. But now another danger arises, as the rest of the poem explains. Unless they can maintain their love at this high point they will begin to deceive each other and thus new shadows of a sadder kind will fall upon their love.

> Except our loves at this noone stay,
> We shall new shadowes make the other way.
> As the first were made to blinde
> Others; these which come behinde
> Will worke upon our selves, and blind our eyes.
> If our loves faint, and westwardly decline;
> To me thou, falsly, thine,
> And I to thee mine actions shall disguise.
> The morning shadowes weare away,
> But these grow longer all the day,
> But oh, loves day is short, if love decay.
>
> Love is a growing, or full constant light;
> And his first minute, after noone, is night.

There is no comfort in this poem, only the presentation of a precarious dilemma. Love's philosophy, it seems, begins with the recognition of the shadow of decay.

We have seen in many of the preceding quotations the constant pressure of Donne's awareness of the shadow of time and death. It is indeed the point from which his poetical "lectures" all arise. Realizing this, one may see a certain propriety in two apparently anomalous poems that appear among the love-songs in the "Group I" manuscripts.[17] Almost exactly in the middle of the forty-seven poems contained in this collection of the love-poems, we find, as the twenty-fifth poem, the elegy entitled "Autumnall" (Grierson's Elegy IX), and two poems later, the curious two-part poem with the general title "Epitaph" and the sub-title "Omnibus." It is natural, of course, to remove the "Autumnall" to a place with the other elegies, since it is clearly entitled "Elegie" and it cannot be called a song or a "sonet" of the kind represented by nearly all the other poems here. And yet, as everyone has noticed, the

"Autumnall" is a poem of quite a different nature from that of the youthful poems that may have composed Donne's "Book of Elegies."[18] It is written in a style unusual for Donne: in a series of end-stopped, frequently-balanced pentameter couplets, a style quite in contrast with the headlong rushing movement of, say, the famous elegy "By our first strange and fatall interview." But this poised and balanced style is appropriate to the poem's theme, which celebrates the beauty of a Lady in her autumnal season:

> Here, where still Evening is; not noone, nor night;
> Where no voluptuousnesse, yet all delight.

This quiet, "tolerable" style helps to create the sense of a beauty delicately poised between passion and death, as Donne indicates by the act of denying the presence of the grave in her brow:

> Call not these wrinkles, graves; If graves they were,
> They were Loves graves; for else he is no where.
> Yet lies not Love dead here, but here doth sit
> Vow'd to this trench, like an Anachorit.
> And here, till hers, which must be his death, come,
> He doth not digge a Grave, but build a Tombe.

She is indeed lovely in her season, and yet the season stands at the far edge of beauty, as Donne realizes near the end of the poem when, with a certain horror, he moves back from the thought of the fate which certainly awaits such beauty:

> If we love things long sought, Age is a thing
> Which we are fifty yeares in compassing.

If transitory things, which soone decay,
Age must be lovelyest at the latest day.
But name not Winter-faces, whose skin's slacke;
Lanke, as an unthrifts purse; but a soules sacke;
Whose Eyes seeke light within, for all here's shade;
Whose mouthes are holes, rather worne out, then made;
Whose every tooth to a'severall place is gone,
To vexe their soules at Resurrection;
Name not these living Deaths-heads unto mee,
For these, not Ancient, but Antiques be.

They are "Antiques," as Miss Gardner explains,[19] in the sense of "antics"—grotesques—fantastic corruptions of humanity. Nevertheless Donne accepts this fate gently at the close of the poem. It is, he says, "loves naturall lation," using an old astrological term that indicates "the action of moving, or the motion of a body from one place to another" (*OED*). It is a phrase worth remembering, for it might be said that Donne's greatest love-poetry represents an effort to create a counteraction to "loves naturall lation."

One may find a similar propriety in the even more anomalous "Epitaph" which appears among the love-songs in three of the "Group I" manuscripts.[20] This neglected poem has had perhaps the most curious history of printing of all Donne's poems: at one time or another, in whole or in part, it has appeared among his funeral elegies, his Divine Poems, his verse letters, or in Grierson's edition, in a section created wholly for itself. The "Epitaph" proper is prefaced by a verse epistle to a Lady:

Madame,
That I might make your Cabinet my tombe,
    And for my fame, which I love next my soule,

> Next to my soule provide the happiest roome,
>   Admit to that place this last funerall Scrowle.
>   Others by Testament give Legacies, but I
>   Dying, of you doe beg a Legacie.

The speaker, in the person of his poem, asks his Lady to take this piece of writing into her "Cabinet," that is, into her boudoir, so that his reputation may reside next to his soul, which already lives in his Lady's intimate presence. Then follows the epitaph addressed to all, including the Lady herself. It is a death's-head, warning the reader to realize that he is himself clay, as the speaker is now within his grave. And so the epitaph concludes:

> Whilst in our soules sinne bred and pamper'd is,
> Our soules become wormeaten carkases;
> So we our selves miraculously destroy.
> Here bodies with lesse miracle enjoy
> Such priviledges, enabled here to scale
> Heaven, when the Trumpets ayre shall them exhale.
> Heare this, and mend thy selfe, and thou mendst me,
> By making me being dead, doe good to thee,
> And thinke me well compos'd, that I could now
> A last-sicke houre to syllables allow.

It is a strange, and yet, with Donne, a characteristic gesture: that he should send his Lady this *memento mori* by which he wishes to be remembered (with a witty turn) as a man "well compos'd," well prepared for death—and still a good poet! It is a gesture quite in line with the passage that I have quoted from Izaak Walton's account of Donne's last illness: that scene where Donne arises from his death-bed to stand upon an urn and strike one final posture in marble. In both actions we may feel, while Donne makes his gesture of renunciation, that there remains a deep longing to maintain an involvement with the physical world, whether that involvement takes the form of a poem kept in his Lady's boudoir or the form of a marble statue preserved in a great Cathedral. In these and many other ways, throughout his poetry, Donne's questing mind reveals and controls the contraries that meet within his being.

II

Thomas Carew

The Cavalier World

Figure 8. "The Emperor Albanactus." Design by Inigo Jones for the role played by Charles I in the masque by Aurelian Townshend, *Albions Triumph*, 1632. (*Devonshire Collection, Chatsworth; reproduced by kind permission of the Trustees of the Chatsworth Settlement. Simpson and Bell,* Designs, No. 124.)

II

Thomas Carew

The Cavalier World

In the cold spring of 1639, Thomas Carew, the favorite poet of the Court of Charles I, joined his King's army in an ill-conceived and ill-prepared expedition against the Scots. It was the same expedition for which Carew's friend and fellow poet, Sir John Suckling, had beggared himself in order to provide a beautifully clothed and plumed troop of cavalrymen—but whether they could fight was another matter. The King's hope was to quell the rebellious Scots, who had refused to abide by the rules of the Church of England; but he found the Scottish army much too strong for his own forces, stronger in motivation, bound together by religious zeal, and therefore stronger in military capacity. Charles did not dare to invade Scotland, and indeed hardly a shot was fired. Instead Charles made a humiliating, temporary peace, and planned to bide his time until, as he hoped, his power would grow stronger. Instead he grew steadily weaker. The Scottish expedition was the beginning of the end of Charles I's regime, an open revelation of the weaknesses that beset his state both in England and in Scotland; thus began a swift decay of royal power that reached its end when, in 1649, the Parliamentary army beheaded the King and abolished his monarchy.

Thomas Carew did not live to see the death of this "brave Prince of Cavaliers," as Robert Herrick called him, for Carew died in March, 1640—a symbolic date, for that was the very spring when Charles was forced to reconvene Parliament after his eleven years of personal rule. Thus began in November, 1640, the Long Parliament which utterly destroyed the King's power.

In the year 1640, shortly before Thomas Carew's death, it seems, he composed a poem in which memories of the Scottish campaign form a dark opening that fades away before an overwhelming appreciation of a way of life that represents the best of the Cavalier ideal: "To my friend G. N. from Wrest"—a country estate in Bedfordshire.

> I Breathe (sweet *Ghib:*) the temperate ayre of *Wrest*
> Where I no more with raging stormes opprest,
> Weare the cold nights out by the bankes of Tweed,
> On the bleake Mountaines, where fierce tempests breed,
> And everlasting Winter dwells; where milde
> *Favonius,* and the Vernall windes exilde,
> Did never spread their wings: but the wilde North
> Brings sterill Fearne, Thistles, and Brambles forth.
> Here steep'd in balmie dew, the pregnant Earth
> Sends from her teeming wombe a flowrie birth,
> And cherisht with the warme Suns quickning heate,
> Her porous bosome doth rich odours sweate;[1]

We should note how, unlike Donne, Carew has a warm appreciation of the natural vigor of the earth. He goes on to admire the simple mansion, not erected "with curious skill" or with "carved Marble, Touch, or Porpherie." This is a house built for hospitality, without Doric or Corinthian pillars; it is designed for service, not for show. In the center of the poem he draws an active picture of the Lord and Lady at the head of "their merry Hall" filled with people of all ranks, servants, tenants, women, steward, chaplain, all eating at various tables in appropriate but flexible hierarchy. Meanwhile "others of better note"

> freely sit
> At the Lords Table, whose spread sides admit
> A large accesse of friends to fill those seates
> Of his capacious circle, fill'd with meates
> Of choycest rellish, till his Oaken back
> Under the load of pil'd-up dishes crack.

Although he praises the house for not being showy with statuary and extravagant artifice, the whole estate nevertheless reveals itself to be a work of art on the outside where nature and art have combined to direct the waters flowing from the local spring. Art, says Carew,

> entertaines the flowing streames in deepe
> And spacious channells, where they slowly creepe
> In snakie windings, as the shelving ground
> Leades them in circles, till they twice surround
> This Island Mansion, which i' th' center plac'd,
> Is with a double Crystall heaven embrac'd . . .

The whole view of the estate, then, is one in which simple dignity and generous hospitality combine with art to create an atmosphere of natural fertility and bounty. This theme reaches a climax in the finale as Carew sees the landscape and the fountain of waters mingled with pastoral and mythological figures out of Ovid's *Metamorphoses* and Vergil's *Georgics:*

> With various Trees we fringe the waters brinke,
> Whose thirstie rootes the soaking moysture drinke,
> And whose extended boughes in equall rankes
> Yeeld fruit, and shade, and beautie to the bankes.
> On this side young *Vertumnus* sits, and courts
> His ruddie-cheek'd *Pomona*, *Zephyre* sports
> On th'other, with lov'd *Flora*, yeelding there
> Sweetes for the smell, sweetes for the palate here.
> But did you taste the high & mighty drinke
> Which from that Fountaine flowes, you'ld cleerly think
> The God of Wine did his plumpe clusters bring,
> And crush the Falerne grape into our spring;
>
> . . . . .
>
> Thus I enjoy my selfe, and taste the fruit
> Of this blest Peace, whilst toyl'd in the pursuit
> Of Bucks, and Stags, th'embleme of warre, you strive
> To keepe the memory of our Armes alive.

Thus the poem is framed by memories of the war, as though the threat of destruction had led Carew to appreciate the values of this ancient, traditional way of noble country life—a way of life celebrated long before by Carew's poetical master and father, Ben Jonson, in his similar poem "Penshurst," and by Jonson's own masters, Vergil, Horace, and Martial.

And indeed had such a way of life really been honored and followed by King Charles and his Court, the monarchy would never have come to its disaster. But by the year 1640 Charles and his Court had lost touch with the common people, unlike the Lord and Lady in their crowded hall at Wrest. Charles and his Court lived more and more a life apart, charmed by art and music, led by a King of impeccable artistic taste, whose collection of works of art, gathered in his palaces, represented one of the greatest art collections in all of Europe. Inigo Jones, that architect of rare ability, was in charge of all the King's buildings; Jones's new banqueting house at

Figure 9. Van Dyck: "Charles I in Three Positions." Painted c. 1635–6 as a basis for the marble bust of Charles made by Bernini in Rome. (*Windsor Castle; reproduced by gracious permission of Her Majesty Queen Elizabeth II.*)

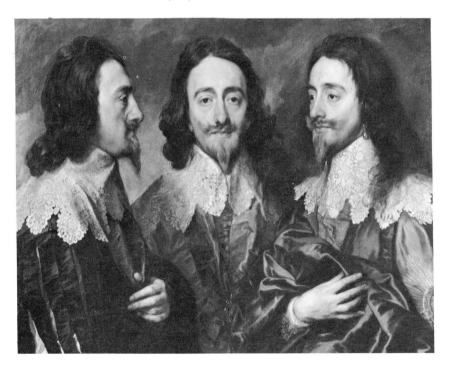

Whitehall, built in the latter years of King James's reign, had its ceiling painted by Rubens during Charles's reign; and Van Dyck came from Antwerp to live as the resident painter of King Charles and his Court. But by the year 1640 this era of courtly elegance and art was near its end.

That end may be seen as symbolized in two more events of this climacteric year: by the publication, in May or June, 1640, a few months after Thomas Carew's death, of his volume of collected poems, containing a world of Cavalier ideals; and secondly, by the presentation, in January, 1640, of the last of the great Court masques, *Salmacida Spolia*, composed jointly by Inigo Jones and by Carew's good friend and fellow poet, Sir William Davenant. The masque was based upon a curious allegorical interpretation of the myth of Salmacis, which is here interpreted as representing "Salmacian spoils," that is to say, rewards gained by peace and not by destructive war. It is the climax and epitome of the great series of Court masques that had flourished during the reign of James I on a relatively simpler scale, and then gradually rose to a scale of greater and greater extravagance after the reign of Charles I began in 1625. The masques of the Caroline era were glorious, expensive spectacles that called upon all the Court's immense artistic resources, for scene designing, for costume, for music, for dancing, and for poetry. All these resources were brought together for the last time in *Salmacida Spolia*, to give a moral allegory of the times, as the published version of the entertainment describes it:[2]

Figure 10. Van Dyck: Charles I, 1636. (*Windsor Castle; reproduced by gracious permission of Her Majesty Queen Elizabeth II.*)

The Subject of the Masque

Discord, a malicious Fury, appears in a storm and by the invocation of malignant spirits, proper to her evil use, having already put most of the world into disorder [a reference to the Thirty Years' War then raging on the Continent], endeavours to disturb these parts, envying the blessings and tranquillity we have long enjoyed.

These incantations are expressed by those spirits in an Antimasque; who on a sudden are surprised and stopped in their motion by a secret power, whose wisdom they tremble at; and depart as foreknowing that wisdom will change all their malicious hope of these disorders into a sudden calm, which after their departure is prepared by a dispersed harmony of music.

This secret wisdom, in the person of the King attended by his Nobles and under the name of Philogenes or Lover of his People, hath his appearance prepared by a Chorus, representing the beloved people, and is instantly discovered environed with those Nobles in the Throne of Honour.

Then the Queen personating the chief heroine, with her martial ladies, is sent down from Heaven by Pallas as a reward of his prudence for reducing the threatening storm into the following calm.

Thus, after a series of fantastic scenes representing various aspects of discord and disorder, the King makes his appearance in great magnificence:

Figure 11. A Masquer. Design by Inigo Jones for *Salmacida Spolia*, 1640; a similar costume was worn by the King in his role as Philogenes. (*Devonshire Collection, Chatsworth; reproduced by kind permission of the Trustees of the Chatsworth Settlement. Simpson and Bell*, Designs, No. 345.)

Then the further part of the scene disappeared, and the King's Majesty and the rest of the masquers were discovered sitting in the Throne of Honour, his Majesty highest in a seat of gold and the rest of the Lords about him. This throne was adorned with palm trees, between which stood statues of the ancient heroes. In the under parts on each side lay captives bound, in several postures, lying on trophies of armours, shields, and antique weapons, all his throne being feigned of goldsmith's work. The habit of his Majesty and the masquers was of watchet, richly embroidered with silver; long stockings set up of white; their caps silver with scrolls of gold and plumes of white feathers.

Then, after a song in praise of the King's virtues, particularly his patience and mercy in view of "those storms the people's giddy fury raise," the Queen descends in an even more magnificent scene.

Whilst the Chorus sung this song, there came softly from the upper part of the heavens a huge cloud of various colours, but pleasant to the sight; which, descending to the midst of the scene, opened, and within it was a transparent brightness of thin exhalations, such as the Gods are feigned to descend in; in the most eminent place of which her Majesty sat, representing the chief heroine, environed with her martial ladies; and from over her head were darted lightsome rays that illuminated her seat; and all the ladies about her participated more or less of that light, as they sat near or further off. This brightness with many streaks of thin vapours about it, such as are seen in a fair evening sky, softly descended; and as it came

Figure 12. Van Dyck: Queen Henrietta Maria, probably 1632. (*Windsor Castle; reproduced by gracious permission of Her Majesty Queen Elizabeth II.*)

near to the earth the seat of Honour by little and little van-
ished, as if it gave way to these heavenly graces. The Queen's
Majesty and her ladies were in Amazonian habits of carnation,
embroidered with silver, with plumed helms, baldrics with
antique swords hanging by their sides—all as rich as might be;
but the strangeness of the habits was most admired.

Thus with song and dance and extravagant splendor the King
and the Queen and the Court persuaded themselves that peace
was still at hand and that the Court would prevail.

One assumes that Thomas Carew must have been present
at this gorgeous spectacle, for he loved these masques and had
himself composed the libretto for a very expensive and elaborate show entitled *Coelum Britannicum*, presented at Court
in 1634. Of this splendid show, Sir Henry Herbert reports:
"It was the noblest masque of my time to this day, the best
poetrye, best scenes, and the best habitts. The kinge and
queene were very well pleasd with my service, and the Q. was
pleasd to tell mee before the king, 'Pour les habits, elle
n'avoit jamais rien vue de si brave.' "[3] The praise was well
deserved, for Carew's book for the masque is one of the most
thoroughly written that we have for any masque of the day.
Indeed the proportion of poetry to scenery appears to be
larger than that found in any other masque of the time except for Milton's Ludlow masque. It consists of an extravagant hymn of praise for the virtues of the royal pair whose
destiny it is to rout all the vices and disorders of the day and
to bring into the three kingdoms of England, Scotland, and
Ireland a perfect peace derived from perfect morality. Thus
after a long series of anti-masques have been performed,
representing the several disorders of existence, the Genius of
the three kingdoms appears and foresees the future:

> Raise from these rockie cliffs, your heads,
> Brave Sonnes, and see where Glory spreads
> Her glittering wings, where Majesty
> Crown'd with sweet smiles, shoots from her eye
> Diffusive joy, where Good and Faire,
> United sit in Honours chayre.
> Call forth your aged Priests, and chrystall streames,
> To warme their hearts, and waves in these bright beames.[4]

Then after a series of such songs of praise, the noblemen appear, gorgeously arrayed, to begin the defeat of evil:

> At this the under-part of the Rocke opens, and out of a Cave are seene to come the Masquers, richly attired like ancient Heroes, the Colours yellow, embroydered with silver, their antique Helmes curiously wrought, and great plumes on the top; before them a troope of young Lords and Noblemens sonnes bearing Torches of Virgin-wax, these were apparelled after the old British fashion in white Coats, embroydered with silver, girt, and full gathered, cut square coller'd, and round caps on their heads, with a white feather wreathen about them; first these dance with their lights in their hands: After which, the Masquers descend into the roome, and dance their entry.[5]

And then after several harmonious songs, the masque concludes by the appearance of seven magnificent allegorical figures: Religion, Truth, Wisdom, Concord, Government, Reputation, and lastly, Eternity, all joining in praise of the glorious virtues of Britain's King and Queen.

The fatal separation of this gorgeous world of art from the world of political actuality is clearly evidenced in a superb poem that Carew had written, probably in January of 1633, to his friend and fellow poet of the Cavaliers, Aurelian

Townshend. Townshend had written a poem to Carew, urging him to write a poetical tribute in honor of Gustavus Adolphus, who had been killed at the battle of Lützen, November 6, 1632. Thus Carew writes "In answer of an Elegiacall Letter upon the death of the King of Sweden from Aurelian Townsend, inviting me to write on that subject":[6]

> Why dost thou sound, my deare *Aurelian*,
> In so shrill accents, from thy *Barbican*,
> A loude allarum to my drowsie eyes,
> Bidding them wake in teares and Elegies
> For mightie *Swedens* fall? Alas! how may
> My Lyrique feet, that of the smooth soft way
> Of Love, and Beautie, onely know the tread,
> In dancing paces celebrate the dead
> Victorious King, or his Majesticke Hearse
> Prophane with th'humble touch of their low verse?
> *Virgil*, nor *Lucan*, no, nor *Tasso* more
> Then both, not *Donne*, worth all that went before,

(Notice his extraordinary admiration for the poetry of Donne.)

> With the united labour of their wit
> Could a just Poem to this subject fit,
> His actions were too mighty to be rais'd

Figure 13 (opposite). A Masquer. Design by Inigo Jones for Carew's *Coelum Britannicum,* 1634. (*Devonshire Collection, Chatsworth; reproduced by kind permission of the Trustees of the Chatsworth Settlement. Simpson and Bell,* Designs, No. 201.)

Figure 14. Head of a Masquer. Design by Inigo Jones for Carew's *Coelum Britannicum,* 1634. *(Devonshire Collection, Chatsworth; reproduced by kind permission of the Trustees of the Chatsworth Settlement. Simpson and Bell,* Designs, No. 207.)

Figure 15 (opposite). A Torch-bearer. Design by Inigo Jones for Carew's *Coelum Britannicum,* 1634. *(Devonshire Collection, Chatsworth; reproduced by kind permission of the Trustees of the Chatsworth Settlement. Simpson and Bell,* Designs, No. 206.)

SEVENTY-SIX

Higher by Verse, let him in prose be prays'd,
In modest faithfull story, which his deedes
Shall turne to Poems:

It sounds like an honest tribute to a great military leader, and
yet as the poem continues a certain ironic tone appears to
arise in the following lines:

And (since 'twas but his Church-yard) let him have
For his owne ashes now no narrower Grave
Then the whole *German* Continents vast wombe,
Whilst all her Cities doe but make his Tombe.

That is to say, Gustavus has made all of Germany a grave-
yard; therefore let him lie there. If we doubt the irony here
the rest of the passage will bear it out:

Let us to supreame providence commit
The fate of Monarchs, which first thought it fit
To rend the Empire from the *Austrian* graspe,
And next from *Swedens*, even when he did claspe

Figure 16. "Fidamira." Design by Inigo Jones for Walter Montagu's play, *The Shepheards Paradise*, 1633. (*Devonshire Collection, Chatsworth; reproduced by kind permission of the Trustees
of the Chatsworth Settlement. Simpson and Bell*, Designs, No. 176.)
   "Those fine, delicate, cool hands keep one away; they are part of the
   'armour' behind which all feeling, directness, and intimacy are shut off.
   They are part and parcel of the 'accessories,' like the rich detail of the
   costumes, the carefully worked jewels and weapons, the architecture and
   sculpture, and the other things that prevent direct contact with the person portrayed." (Hauser, *Mannerism*, I, 200; referring to Bronzino.)

Fidamira.

> Within his dying armes the Soveraigntie
> Of all those Provinces, that men might see
> The Divine wisedome would not leave that Land
> Subject to any one Kings sole command.

It is clear that Carew is finding no great virtues in military conquest, and quickly he turns his mind to things upon which he places a much higher and indeed a supreme value:

> But let us that in myrtle bowers sit
> Under secure shades, use the benefit
> Of peace and plenty, which the blessed hand
> Of our good King gives this obdurate Land . . .

By the word "obdurate" Carew recognizes that the King is having some difficulty with his subjects, but the passage breathes not the slightest doubt that the King will prevail:

> Let us of Revels sing, and let thy breath
> (Which fill'd Fames trumpet with *Gustavus* death,
> Blowing his name to heaven) gently inspire
> Thy past'rall pipe, till all our swaines admire
> Thy song and subject, whilst they both comprise
> The beauties of the *SHEPHERDS PARADISE:*

Carew is referring here to a pastoral comedy written by his friend Walter Montagu, played (with splendid scenery and costumes) by Queen Henrietta Maria and her Ladies on January 9, 1633, and apparently repeated on February 2, 1633.[7] But the production that Carew now proceeds to describe in his poem is not *The Shepheards Paradise* as we know it from

Figure 17. "A Wood called Love's Cabinet." Design by Inigo Jones for Walter Montagu's play, *The Shepheards Paradise*, 1633; Act V: the setting for an important episode played by the Queen in her role as Bellesa. (*Devonshire Collection, Chatsworth; reproduced by kind permission of the Trustees of the Chatsworth Settlement. Simpson and Bell*, Designs, No. 167.)

the printed text of 1659; instead, as Dunlap has pointed out,[8] Carew's description suggests the masque *Tempe Restord*, which Aurelian Townshend and Inigo Jones had presented in February, 1632. Carew urges his friend to continue writing works in the pastoral genre, "For who like thee," Carew asks,

> In sweetly-flowing numbers may advance
> The glorious night? When, not to act foule rapes,
> Like birds, or beasts, but in their Angel-shapes
> A troope of Deities came downe to guide
> Our steerelesse barkes in passions swelling tide
> By vertues Carde, and brought us from above
> A patterne of their owne celestiall love.

With that echo of the concluding lines of Donne's "Canonization," Carew seems to be describing the elaborate descent of "Divine Beauty" and the "Stars," in *Tempe Restord*, as the Queen and her Ladies descended in one of Inigo Jones's miraculous machines and brought home to earth the meaning of true virtue as opposed to Circean corruption.[9] And this resemblance is borne out by Carew's reference to "the divine

Figure 18 (opposite). "Influences of the Stars." Design by Inigo Jones for *Tempe Restord*, 1632: "*Harmony* comes foorth attended by a *Chorus* of Musique, and under her conduct fourteene Influences of the stars, which are to come." Townshend, *Poems and Masks*, ed. Chambers, p. 88. (*Devonshire Collection, Chatsworth; reproduced by kind permission of the Trustees of the Chatsworth Settlement. Simpson and Bell*, Designs, No. 158.)
". . . the ostentatious grace, the affectation and desire to please . . . and the taste for the artificial and unspontaneous that here leads to characteristic mannerist dance poses, are pushed a stage further." (Hauser, *Mannerism*, I, 183; referring to Pontormo.)

Venus" and "her heavenly *Cupid*" in the following lines, for in *Tempe Restord* the appearance of the Queen and her Ladies is praised for creating an "Ayre" "Where faire and good, inseparably conioynd,/Create a *Cupid*, that is never blind."[10] Thus Carew continues:

> Nor lay it in darke sullen precepts drown'd
> But with rich fancie, and cleare Action crown'd
> Through a misterious fable (that was drawne
> Like a transparant veyle of purest Lawne
> Before their dazelling beauties) the divine
> *Venus*, did with her heavenly *Cupid* shine.
> The stories curious web, the Masculine stile,
> The subtile sence, did Time and sleepe beguile,
> Pinnion'd and charm'd they stood to gaze upon
> Th'Angellike formes, gestures, and motion,
> To heare those ravishing sounds that did dispence
> Knowledge and pleasure, to the soule, and sense.

So far the parallel may seem to fit; but the conclusion of Carew's account describes two events for which there is no real correspondence in *Tempe Restord*. At the close of this masque Cupid simply flies up into the air,[11] but Carew describes a much more elaborate action that suggests the Platonizing theme of Montagu's play:[12]

Figure 19 (opposite). "Divine Beauty" and "Stars." Design by Inigo Jones for roles played by the Queen and her Ladies in *Tempe Restord*, 1632: "in a garment of watchet Sattine with Stars of silver imbrodered and imbost from the ground, and on her head a Crowne of Stars mixt with some small falls of white Feathers." Townshend, *Poems and Masks*, ed. Chambers, pp. 91–2. (*Devonshire Collection, Chatsworth; reproduced by kind permission of the Trustees of the Chatsworth Settlement. Simpson and Bell, Designs, No. 161.*)

It fill'd us with amazement to behold
Love made all spirit, his corporeall mold
Dissected into Atomes melt away
To empty ayre, and from the grosse allay
Of mixtures, and compounding Accidents
Refin'd to immateriall Elements.

And finally, Carew makes the Queen's own singing the climax
of his account, whereas in *Tempe Restord* the Queen does
not sing:

But when the Queene of Beautie did inspire
The ayre with perfumes, and our hearts with fire,
Breathing from her celestiall Organ sweet
Harmonious notes, our soules fell at her feet,
And did with humble reverend dutie, more
Her rare perfections, then high state adore.

In the fifth Act of *The Shepheards Paradise*, however, a song of
twenty lines is sung by the Queen in her role as Bellesa, chosen
for her beauty as "Queen" of this pastoral retreat. Immediately after this she falls asleep, being alone, and Moramente
enters, "sees her here lie sleeping and stands wondering,"
with the following speech:

Was it the rapture my soule was allwayes in, when
she contemplates the divine *Bellesa*, that did present
her voyce unto me here in heaven? Sure it was: her
soul, uselesse now unto her body, is gon to visit
heaven, and did salute the Angels with a song.[13]

Figure 20. Queen Henrietta Maria as "Divine Beauty" in *Tempe Restord*, 1632. Miniature by John Hoskins. (*Royal Library, Windsor Castle; reproduced by gracious permission of Her Majesty Queen Elizabeth II. Photo by courtesy of Messrs. Sotheby and Co.*)

These words of Moramente seem to "comprise" the subject for a song that appears in Townshend's collected works, with the title "On his Hearing her Majesty sing":

I have beene in Heav'n, I thinke,
For I heard an Angell sing,
Notes my thirsty ears did drinke.
Never any earthly thing
Sung so true, so sweet, so cleere;
I was then in Heav'n, not heere.

But the blessed feele no change,
So I may mistake the place,
But mine eyes would think it strange,
Should that be no Angels face;
Pow'rs above, it seems, designe
Me still Mortall, her Divine.

Till I tread the Milky way,
And I lose my sences quite,
All I wish is that I may
Hear that voice, and see that sight,
Then in types and outward show
I shall have a Heav'n below.[14]

It seems possible that this song may have formed a part of
some adaptation of *The Shepheards Paradise*. And there is
evidence that such an adaptation was made. A manuscript in
the Folger Library represents an acting version of *The Shepheards Paradise*, with a prologue and certain songs between
the acts which do not appear in the printed text of the play.[15]
This prologue makes it plain that some kind of masque is
being presented in coordination with Montagu's play, certainly at the beginning, and possibly between the acts as well.
The prologue presents Apollo and Diana in conversation;
Apollo tells Diana that the Gods have agreed to appear on
this occasion in the form of stars:

> Soe now by this they all consented are,
> Each one to put himselfe into a starre:
> And thus in Gallantry each brings a light,
> And waites with it a servant to this night,
> They'le give the light & leave you to preside
> In vertue, but as you are Deifide;

Perhaps the Gods then, later in the evening, descended from their Heaven and appeared in the manner described in Carew's lines above:

> When, not to act foule rapes,
> Like birds, or beasts, but in their Angel-shapes
> A troope of Deities came downe to guide
> Our steerelesse barkes in passions swelling tide
> By vertues Carde . . .

Certainly these lines accord much better with the Gods and stars of the prologue than they do with the descent of the Queen and her Ladies as stars in *Tempe Restord*. Has Townshend perhaps used some of the themes, along with the costumes, settings, and machinery, from his masque of the previous year, in order to enhance the beauties of *The Shepheards Paradise*?[16] It seems likely, all considered, and such a conclusion would resolve the puzzle of Carew's account, which seems to describe a production related to *The Shepheards Paradise*, and yet devised in some manner by Townshend as well. In any case, such are the "pastimes" that Carew asks his friend to celebrate, as he ends the poem to Townshend with these most significant and revealing lines:

These harmelesse pastimes let my *Townsend* sing
To rurall tunes; not that thy Muse wants wing
To soare a loftier pitch, for she hath made
A noble flight, and plac'd th'Heroique shade
Above the reach of our faint flagging ryme;
But these are subjects proper to our clyme.
Tourneyes, Masques, Theaters, better become
Our *Halcyon* dayes; what though the German Drum
Bellow for freedome and revenge, the noyse
Concernes not us, nor should divert our joyes;
Nor ought the thunder of their Carabins
Drowne the sweet Ayres of our tun'd Violins;
Beleeve me friend, if their prevailing powers
Gaine them a calme securitie like ours,
They'le hang their Armes up on the Olive bough,
And dance, and revell then, as we doe now.

The whole situation of the Cavalier world, as glimpsed in this poem, and indeed the full impact of Carew's poetry, may be seen as symbolized in a great Mannerist painting by Bronzino, of which I was reminded by reading *The Nice and the Good* by Iris Murdoch, who has given this painting a symbolic place in her book. It is Bronzino's allegory known as "Venus, Cupid, Folly, and Time," where the graceful, harmonious, beautifully posed figure of Venus forms the center of the picture, while her grace is threatened from all sides by corrupting forces. Her son, Cupid, kneels beside her on the left in a distorted posture, embracing her indecently. Old Father Time holds over the head of Venus a threatening muscular arm. On the right side dances the figure of Folly

Figure 21 (opposite). Bronzino: "Venus, Cupid, Folly, and Time." (*National Gallery, London; reproduced by kind permission of the Trustees of the National Gallery.*)

or Pleasure, a young boy with a glint of madness in his eyes. In the background, darkened in shadows, lurk three sinister figures: one in the upper left corner may represent the figure of Truth, who seems to be turning her face away in horror from the scene; down lower on the left one sees clearly the tormented face of a figure that must be Jealousy; and in the background on the right side lurks a strange composite monster who must be the figure of Deceit, for the bland, pretty face does not square with the animal lower parts that we can see in the corner of the painting; moreover, as critics point out, her left and right hands are misplaced.[17] Can the Queen of Love and Beauty survive these threats?

Thomas Carew is not wholly unaware of these dangers, for his poems deal incessantly with time, infidelity, and death. Many of his finest poems are funeral tributes or poems written to the King or to noble ladies when they are suffering illness. Here, for example, is a poem where the images of red and white common to love-poetry are turned gracefully to deal with the paleness of a young lady suffering from some anemic disease:

Stay coward blood, and doe not yield
To thy pale sister, beauties field,
Who there displaying round her white
Ensignes, hath usurp'd thy right;
Invading thy peculiar throne,
The lip, where thou shouldst rule alone;
And on the cheeke, where natures care
Allotted each an equall share,
Her spreading Lilly only growes,
Whose milky deluge drownes thy Rose.

> Quit not the field faint blood, nor rush
> In the short salley of a blush,
> Upon thy sister foe, but strive
> To keepe an endlesse warre alive;
> Though peace doe petty States maintaine,
> Here warre alone makes beauty raigne.

But sometimes Death will win, as Carew shows in a poem on the death of a young girl, Lady Mary Villers, where all the symbols of Love and Beauty are delicately brought together in balanced, measured form to pay a tribute to the death of youth:

> This little Vault, this narrow roome,
> Of Love, and Beautie is the tombe;
> The dawning beame that 'gan to cleare
> Our clouded skie, lyes darkned here,
> For ever set to us, by death
> Sent to enflame the world beneath;
> 'Twas but a bud, yet did containe
> More sweetnesse then shall spring againe,
> A budding starre that might have growne
> Into a Sun, when it had blowne.
> This hopefull beautie, did create
> New life in Loves declining state;
> But now his Empire ends, and we
> From fire, and wounding darts are free:
> His brand, his bow, let no man feare,
> The flames, the arrowes, all lye here.

It seems appropriate to call this poem a work of Mannerist art, if we do not use the term Mannerist in a derogatory sense. I will use it as many art historians do, when they seek to describe certain aspects of late Renaissance culture, during the last seventy years or so of the sixteenth century, the period after the death of the two great masters, Raphael and Leonardo. But we must define closely the term Mannerist, as John Shearman has tried to do in his recent book on this subject.[18] As he and many others have pointed out, "Mannerism" is derived from the Italian word *maniera*, meaning simply, *style*. A Mannerist painter is a painter with high style, with so strong an emphasis on style that it stands out as the figure of Venus stands out in Bronzino's painting among the threatening gestures of the other figures in the scene. A Mannerist painter has learned all that can be learned from the earlier great masters and he now proceeds to turn their art and craft toward other ends, creating a different kind of art in which the high style stands at the front, taking the eye with its elegance and its sophistication. Such art can, of course, be mere imitation in the bad sense of that word, but it may also be creative imitation—that is, imitation of the manner of the great masters which moves into a different era of sensibility and creates a new world of art. Now transferring cautiously this term into the poetic realm, perhaps we might say that Carew is a Mannerist because he imitates so skillfully the works of the great masters who preceded him and yet brings their art into a different dimension, celebrating values different from those presented by Donne and Jonson and other poets to whom Carew is obviously indebted. The short epitaph that I have just read inherits the Jonsonian form as displayed in many of Jonson's own epigrams and epitaphs, but carries beyond Jonson its elegance and perfection of form, its delicacy of sympathetic admiration for dead Beauty.

Carew's admiration for his master, Ben Jonson, is no empty adulation, as we may see from the remarkable poem that Carew wrote to Ben on the occasion of his poetical father's outrageous exhibition of bad temper when the public hissed his play, *The New Inn*, off the stage in 1629.[19] In 1631 Jonson published the play with a title-page in which he blames everybody but himself for the failure:

> A Comoedy. As it was never acted, but most
> negligently play'd, by some, the Kings Servants.
> And more squeamishly beheld, and censured by
> others, the Kings Subjects. 1629. Now, at last,
> set at liberty to the Readers, his Majesties
> Servants, and Subjects, to be judg'd.

He appends to the play a very bad-tempered poem in which he denounces the English audience in these words:

> Come leave the lothed stage,
>   And the more lothsome age:
> Where pride, and impudence (in faction knit)
>   Usurpe the chaire of wit!
> Indicting, and arraigning every day
>   Something they call a Play.
>   Let their fastidious, vaine
>   Commission of the braine
> Run on, and rage, sweat, censure, and condem'n:
> They were not made for thee, lesse, thou for them.

Carew pays his master Ben the ultimate tribute by judging this outburst of temper in strict accordance with the master's own principles. Carew's poem acts as a tacit reminder that Jonson has urged the use of reason and proportion, that he has represented the values of balance and self-control—the

virtues of Roman poetry and of Roman morality. The poem
is friendly, but judicious, gentle, but firm:

> Tis true (deare *Ben*:) thy just chastizing hand
> Hath fixt upon the sotted Age a brand
> To their swolne pride, and empty scribbling due,
> It can nor judge, nor write, and yet 'tis true
> Thy commique Muse from the exalted line
> Toucht by thy *Alchymist*, doth since decline
> From that her Zenith, and foretells a red
> And blushing evening, when she goes to bed,
> Yet such, as shall out-shine the glimmering light
> With which all stars shall guild the following night.

We should notice that Carew is paying a brilliant tribute
to his master here by writing his poem in the style of Jonson's
verse epistles, a style sufficiently end-stopped to keep the
couplet form alive, and observing the caesura frequently, in
good classical form with an effect of balance and proportion, and yet with a movement flexible enough to allow for
the colloquial idiom of a good verse-letter. At the same time
Carew reveals here his fine critical sense, recognizing that
Jonson had reached the peak of his power in the *Alchemist*,
produced nearly twenty years before. He chides his father
by saying that of course an author may very well bind "In
equall shares thy love on all thy race;" nevertheless it is the
reader's duty to "distinguish of their sexe, and place;"

> Though one hand form them, & though one brain strike
> Soules into all, they are not all alike.
> Why should the follies then of this dull age
> Draw from thy Pen such an immodest rage

> As seemes to blast thy (else-immortall) Bayes,
> When thine owne tongue proclaimes thy ytch of praise?

And he urges his master to continue his learned use of materials from ancient authors, and says that no one should

> thinke it theft, if the rich spoyles so torne
> From conquered Authors, be as Trophies worne—

thus defending Jonson against the charge of plagiarism from ancient authors, a charge often leveled against him. In one phrase he sums up the essence of Jonsonian technique:

> Repine not at the Tapers thriftie waste,
> That sleekes thy terser Poems . . .

Terser is the exact word to describe the essence of Jonsonian art, for *terse* means not simply concise and compact, but it means, in Elizabethan English, polished, brilliant, sleeked, burnished by careful craftsmanship.

Such then is Carew's critical admiration for one of the old masters, even in that master's declining years. But there were other masters. One of them has inspired what is perhaps Carew's greatest poem: "An Elegie upon the death of the Deane of Pauls, Dr. John Donne." Here Carew sums up Donne's achievement with a critical acumen never surpassed in later critical writings: if we grasp the poem we grasp Donne. Carew saw, as well as T. S. Eliot, Donne's power of feeling his thought as immediately as the odor of a rose; he saw as well as Grierson Donne's immense power of "passionate ratiocination" where image and argument are compressed in one dramatic moment:

> But the flame
> Of thy brave Soule, (that shot such heat and light,
> As burnt our earth, and made our darknesse bright,
> Committed holy Rapes upon our Will,
> Did through the eye the melting heart distill;
> And the deepe knowledge of darke truths so teach,
> As sense might judge, what phansie could not reach;)
> Must be desir'd for ever.

And we note that Carew here surpasses all other critical essays on Donne by creating his essay in Donne's own style, with the enormous suspension of syntax over-riding the couplet form in the manner of Donne's long passionate utterances. He praises Donne for refusing to imitate ancient authors and for using the English language in a remarkably original fashion that enabled Donne to excel poets who were born to speak languages more musical than English—languages such as Latin or Italian, "whose tun'd chime/More charmes the outward sense."

> Yet thou maist claime
> From so great disadvantage greater fame,
> Since to the awe of thy imperious wit
> Our stubborne language bends, made only fit
> With her tough-thick-rib'd hoopes to gird about
> Thy Giant phansie, which had prov'd too stout
> For their soft melting Phrases.

Here the phrase "imperious wit" strikes to the very center of Donne's achievement, for Carew is using *wit* here in the broad seventeenth-century sense, meaning creative intellect, along with all the other associations that wit has in our own day.

Donne's *imperious* intellect, his indomitable reason, bends
our stubborn language into forms unprecedented in earlier
ages, creating those extraordinary stanza forms that Donne
used for one poem and one poem only. We should note here
that Carew is praising Donne in a way that seems to castigate
himself, for Carew well knows that he himself is a writer of
"soft melting Phrases" and that he himself has brought back
into poetry the kind of mythological imagery which he praises
Donne for having banished from English verse:

> But thou art gone, and thy strict lawes will be
> Too hard for Libertines in Poetrie.
> They will repeale the goodly exil'd traine
> Of gods and goddesses, which in thy just raigne
> Were banish'd nobler Poems, now, with these
> The silenc'd tales o'th' Metamorphoses
> Shall stuffe their lines, and swell the windy Page,
> Till Verse refin'd by thee, in this last Age
> Turne ballad rime, Or those old Idolls bee
> Ador'd againe, with new apostasie;

And Carew then concludes by lines that celebrate the end of
an era, appropriately echoing both Shakespeare and Donne,[20]
as his Elegy proclaims

> The death of all the Arts, whose influence
> Growne feeble, in these panting numbers lies
> Gasping short winded Accents, and so dies:
> So doth the swiftly turning wheele not stand
> In th'instant we withdraw the moving hand,
> But some small time maintaine a faint weake course
> By vertue of the first impulsive force:

Thus Carew, writing shortly after Donne's death in 1631, grasps both the style and the deep significance of Donne's poetical achievement. Carew is indeed one of the great critics of English literature; if he had been writing in our own day he would undoubtedly be known as one of the "new critics."

The extraordinary Mannerist quality that Carew has, in imitating to perfection the style of the great masters, is shown with equal strength in another "critical essay" that he wrote, "To my worthy friend Master Geo. Sands, on his translation of the Psalmes," as the title reads in Carew's collected poems. Here is another poem in pentameter couplets, but we notice that the style does not display either the moderate, flexibly end-stopped movement of Jonson's verse epistles, nor the passionate rush of Donne's over-riding Muse:

> I presse not to the Quire, nor dare I greet
> The holy place with my unhallowed feet;
> My unwasht Muse, polutes not things Divine,
> Nor mingles her prophaner notes with thine;
> Here, humbly at the porch she listning stayes,
> And with glad eares sucks in thy sacred layes.
> So, devout penitents of Old were wont,
> Some without dore, and some beneath the Font,
> To stand and heare the Churches Liturgies,
> Yet not assist the solemne exercise:
> Sufficeth her, that she a lay-place gaine,
> To trim thy Vestments, or but beare thy traine;
> Though nor in tune, nor wing, she reach thy Larke,
> Her Lyrick feet may dance before the Arke.

These couplets are completely end-stopped, each couplet standing as a perfect unit, somewhat anticipating the Augustan manner in caesura, balance, and antithesis. Carew is presenting here a superb imitation of the couplet style that George Sandys had achieved in his famous translation of Ovid's *Metamorphoses*, published in 1626, and widely regarded by modern scholars as a very important step in the creation of the couplet form mastered by Dryden and Pope.[21] Equally important, one should note that exactly this kind of closed couplet also covers many pages in the volume, *A Paraphrase Upon the Divine Poems*, by George Sandys, in which Carew's poem first appeared, in 1638, headed simply "To my worthy friend Mr. George Sandys." Carew is not thinking only of the Psalms here, although Sandys did translate eighteen of the Psalms in this volume into pentameter couplets; but the volume also contains enormous paraphrases of other books of the Bible, such as the fifty-five-page paraphrase of the Book of Job with which the volume opens, done in the closed couplet form. As usual, Carew is fitting the style of his essay to the form of the poetry that he is celebrating.

What we see then in these three poems to three early masters, Jonson, Donne, and Sandys, is Carew's critical ability to enter into the very world created by other poets, to absorb them, understand them, and recreate them in his own mind—surely the basic quality that one expects in any good critic. But Carew's critical sense is best shown by his realization of the limitations of his own Muse, which, as he says, is made to sing the cause of Love and Beauty, as indeed he has done for the whole Cavalier Court. A great many of Carew's poems are entitled "Song" and rightly so, for dozens of them were set to music by the best musicians at the Court of Charles I. Some sixty musical settings for his Songs have been discovered[22]— most of them by Henry Lawes, the chief composer of the day in England, the man who composed the music for Milton's masque in 1634, who in fact directed the masque and played the part of Thyrsis in it. In 1634, Carew and Milton were both participating in the Mannerist art of the Cavalier Court; and indeed the two Egerton boys, who played in Milton's masque, had played only a few months before in Carew's masque *Coelum Britannicum*. The great divisions that were soon to split all England had not yet appeared within the world of art.

In these love songs Carew is working in the great European tradition of the courtly love-lyric, inspired by all the Italian love-poets from Petrarch down to Carew's contemporary Marino, and also inspired by many French poets of the sixteenth century.[23] It is important to remember that Charles's Queen, Henrietta Maria, was a Frenchwoman, the daughter of a Medici, and that she brought with her into England an affection for the graceful beauty of French and Italian art-forms, from which the Court masque indeed derives. These European courtly analogues outweigh any echoes that may be assembled from Donne or even from Jonson. Certainly Carew owes something to Donne and distinct echoes of Donne's poems can easily be found, as in his poem, "Upon a Ribband," in which he echoes Donne's famous conceit, "A bracelet of bright haire about the bone," used by Donne in "The Funerall" and in "The Relique." But significantly, this macabre image, combining a symbol of physical love with a symbol of death, is turned by Carew into a graceful compliment. The bracelet here is no longer a "wreath of haire," but is simply a ribbon, a "silken wreath," tied gracefully about the poet's wrist. It is a symbol of what happened to Donne's inspiration when it entered into Carew's realm celebrating the Queen of Love and Beauty:

> This silken wreath, which circles in mine arme,
> Is but an Emblem of that mystique charme,
> Wherewith the magique of your beauties binds
> My captive soule, and round about it winds
> Fetters of lasting love; This hath entwind
> My flesh alone, That hath empalde my mind:
> Time may weare out These soft weak bands; but Those
> Strong chaines of brasse, Fate shall not discompose.
> This holy relique may preserve my wrist,
> But my whole frame doth by That power subsist:

Appropriately, the first five lines of the poem have something of the run-on movement of Donne's dynamic rhythms, but in the last five lines above, we notice that the verse-form gradually modulates into the courtly, Jonsonian mode of the pentameter couplet. The extravagant preoccupation with Donne's influence that marked literary criticism in the earlier years of the twentieth century has led to the listing of Carew in standard bibliographies and anthologies of "The Metaphysical Poets;" yet, as the above poem indicates, the word "metaphysical" will apply only to some of the surface aspects of Carew's work, and even then in only a few of his poems. Songs such as "Ingratefull beauty threatned" or "To my inconstant Mistris" clearly show the accent and the rigorous realism of Donne's dramatic addresses to his Lady:

> Know, *Celia*, (since thou art so proud,)
> 'Twas I that gave thee thy renowne:

Thou hadst, in the forgotten crowd
    Of common beauties, liv'd unknowne,
Had not my verse exhal'd thy name,
And with it, ympt the wings of fame.

      *   *   *   *   *

Tempt me with such affrights no more,
    Lest what I made, I uncreate;
Let fooles thy mystique formes adore,
    I'le know thee in thy mortall state:
Wise Poets that wrap't Truth in tales,
Knew her themselves, through all her vailes.

It has the ring of Donne about it, and yet the Lady's name, Celia, used in many of Carew's poems, links the poem also with the tradition of the Sons of Ben Jonson. The examples of both Donne and Jonson are present in this poem; both poets cooperated in giving Carew's lyrics this quality of terse, colloquial speech. But such a poem as this is quite unusual in Carew's work—there are only four or five other songs which might be found thus to combine the movement of Donne and Jonson. Most of Carew's lyrics are drawn from the courtly world of the whole European Renaissance. This is especially true of Carew's famous erotic poem, "A Rapture," where he urges his Celia in cadences that strongly echo Donne in many places, and yet the total effect of the poem does not at all create the world that we know from Donne's Elegies. Carew's poem achieves success and even a sense of purity, through Carew's delicate use of traditional pastoral images, all imbued with a sense of nature's deep vitality:

Meane while the bubbling streame shall court the shore,
Th'enamoured chirping Wood-quire shall adore
In varied tunes the Deitie of Love;

The gentle blasts of Westerne winds, shall move
The trembling leaves, & through their close bows breath
Still Musick, whilst we rest our selves beneath
Their dancing shade; till a soft murmure, sent
From soules entranc'd in amorous languishment
Rowze us, and shoot into our veines fresh fire,
Till we, in their sweet extasie expire.
    Then, as the empty Bee, that lately bore,
Into the common treasure, all her store,
Flyes 'bout the painted field with nimble wing,
Deflowring the fresh virgins of the Spring;
So will I rifle all the sweets, that dwell
In my delicious Paradise, and swell
My bagge with honey, drawne forth by the power
Of fervent kisses, from each spicie flower.

Thus it seems appropriate that the editor of Carew's volume of 1640 should have chosen as the first poem "The Spring" (and we might remember and contrast it with Donne's "Spring" poem "Loves Growth"). Here in Carew's poem is none of Donne's passionate reasoning, none of Donne's philosophical argumentation and racy wit. Carew's poem is composed in courtly cadences with a perfection of Mannerist elegance, in couplets marked with strong caesurae; indeed the whole poem is poised upon a major caesura in the center, for it is a poem of twenty-four lines which pauses and gracefully turns in another direction exactly in the middle of its thirteenth line. In its Cavalier elegance, its Mannerist styling, with all its subtle harmonies of sound, it draws together themes celebrated in dozens of French, Italian, and English poems of the earlier Renaissance, pastoral, and Petrarchan. But here is the poem in all its perfection:

Now that the winter's gone, the earth hath lost
Her snow-white robes, and now no more the frost
Candies the grasse, or castes an ycie creame
Upon the silver Lake, or Chrystall streame:
But the warme Sunne thawes the benummed Earth,
And makes it tender, gives a sacred birth
To the dead Swallow; wakes in hollow tree
The drowzie Cuckow, and the Humble-Bee.
Now doe a quire of chirping Minstrels bring
In tryumph to the world, the youthfull Spring.
The Vallies, hills, and woods, in rich araye,
Welcome the comming of the long'd for May.
Now all things smile; onely my *Love* doth lowre:
Nor hath the scalding Noon-day-Sunne the power,
To melt that marble yce, which still doth hold
Her heart congeald, and makes her pittie cold.
The Oxe which lately did for shelter flie
Into the stall, doth now securely lie
In open fields; and love no more is made
By the fire side; but in the cooler shade
Amyntas now doth with his *Cloris* sleepe
Under a Sycamoure, and all things keepe
Time with the season, only shee doth carry
Iune in her eyes, in her heart *Ianuary*.

But whether the mistress represents June or January, it appears
that she is equally beautiful, since the beauty of the winter
is clearly being presented in a lovely manner in the first few
lines, and certainly the appreciation of nature suggests the
natural vitality that lurks within the Lady's eyes. And the
same is true of the entire poem: it is a graceful creation in
which a few touches of natural vigor suffice to prevent the
Mannerist perfection from falling into frigidity.

Finally, we may find all these forces, love-songs of the European Renaissance, the craftsmanship of Jonson, and something even perhaps of the metaphysical note of Donne, in Carew's most famous poem, properly entitled simply "A Song":

> Aske me no more where Iove bestowes,
> When Iune is past, the fading rose:
> For in your beauties orient deepe,
> These flowers as in their causes, sleepe.

As readers have often pointed out, the word *causes* adds to the poem a metaphysical note that carries the poem beyond the range of the usual Cavalier lyric, for it evokes Aristotle's doctrine of the four causes: formal, material, efficient, and final (purposive), all of which are contained in the Lady's beauty.

> Aske me no more whether doth stray,
> The golden Atomes of the day:
> For in pure love heaven did prepare
> Those powders to inrich your haire.

> Aske me no more whether doth hast,
> The Nightingale when May is past:
> For in your sweet dividing throat,
> She winters and keepes warme her note.

> Aske me no more where those starres light,
> That downewards fall in dead of night:
> For in your eyes they sit, and there,
> Fixed become as in their sphere.

Aske me no more if East or West,
The Phenix builds her spicy nest:
For unto you at last shee flies,
And in your fragrant bosome dyes.

We notice how these stanzas move from the "golden Atomes" of daylight through the wintering song of the nightingale and into certain suggestions of death and falling in the third stanza—a movement from light to dark, from life to death, summed up in the final stanza where the Phoenix image provides a symbol of both death and resurrection. Thus the poem has, after all, something of the metaphysical movement from the Many toward the One. Here, of course, all is treated in a tone of courtly compliment, but nevertheless with something of Donne's manner of turning all transient images of the Many toward the Oneness that he seeks in his love. The sense of change and death is controlled by turning all things toward the *causes* of his love, and this in miniature is Donne's effect.

In miniature, Carew displays a perfection of form and manner that Donne and Jonson themselves never quite achieved with their more robust and wide-ranging powers; thus Carew's whole volume of 1640 may be said to represent the ideals of the Cavalier world in a series of poetical miniatures, graceful, elegant, perfectly crafted, perfectly absorbing

Figure 22 (opposite). A Masquer. Design by Inigo Jones for an unidentified masque. (*Devonshire Collection, Chatsworth; reproduced by kind permission of the Trustees of the Chatsworth Settlement. Simpson and Bell*, Designs, No. 420.)
"The picture shows . . . not only his elegant, highly-strung, highly-bred human type . . . his freely flowing line and effortless form, but also the subtlety with which he renders the provocative, erotic charm of his figures." (Hauser, *Mannerism*, I, 205; referring to Parmigianino.)

the lessons of the earlier masters. It is a world of art-forms, too fragile to sustain the violent pressures of the times. But in the paintings of Van Dyck, in the drawings of Inigo Jones, and in the poetry of Carew and his friends, those forms of art survive the ashes of political disaster.

III

Richard Crashaw

Love's Architecture

Figure 23. Bernini: *Baldacchino.* (*Photo: Giordani.*)

III

Richard Crashaw

Love's Architecture

During the course of the previous lectures we have moved from the time of that earliest portrait of John Donne, in 1591, down to the time of the death of Charles I, in 1649, the victory of the Cromwellian forces, and the establishment of the Puritan Commonwealth. This entire stretch of sixty years was a period of threatening conflict, both from within, and from foreign enemies, and the era ended in violent Civil War. And yet it was also, we must remember, the time that saw the publication of Spenser's *Faerie Queene*, the writing of all the plays of Shakespeare, and the writing of the earlier poems of John Milton, to say nothing of the works of Donne and Jonson and all the others. It was indeed a time of Renaissance, when London might be said without exaggeration to have rivalled Athens in the time of the great Greek dramatists, or Florence in the age of the Medici. It was a time when all the great currents of revival that had grown up gradually on the Continent over a period of more than two hundred years suddenly flowered in England, within this brief era. As a result, all the styles and stages of the European Renaissance were compressed and recapitulated in England during this brief time. Even more than on the Continent, the phases of style that we call Renaissance, Mannerist, or Baroque all flow together and in England become inseparably intermingled and simultaneous, because of the peculiar compression of the forces of the Renaissance during the first half of the seventeenth century.

I have suggested that Thomas Carew is an English Mannerist, a poet who brought to perfection a special emphasis on style, on the manner, the *maniera*, introduced by earlier masters, especially Donne and Jonson. And I suspect, picking up the suggestion of Roy Daniells,[1] that if John Milton had died in 1650 at the age of 42, with nothing written but those earlier poems published in one volume in 1645, Milton too might have been thought of as a fine Mannerist writer, experimenting in various styles: sonnets, the Court Masque, the Spenserian style (as in his Nativity Ode), the Jonsonian style (as in *L'Allegro* and *Il Penseroso*), a poet who was only beginning to show his greatness in one poem of that highly experimental volume: *Lycidas*, his first great venture in the Baroque idiom, and the poem in which he comes closest to Crashaw.

It is essential now to define what we mean by the term Baroque. I can do so only by beginning with some examples, great and small, from the seventeenth-century visual arts. First of all, let us consider the great *Baldacchino* of Bernini, which stands over the altar under the great dome of St. Peter's in Rome: a massive, elaborately decorated canopy, supported by huge bronze columns covered with gold. Viewed in and by itself, close-up, it may seem an awkward, unstable, and be-

Figure 24. Bernini: *Baldacchino.* (*Photo: Alinari.*)

wildering construction. Yet to see it thus is to mistake its function and effect, for it is not designed to be viewed in and by itself. First of all, seen from the nave, it acts as a frame for the "Cathedra" of St. Peter, as Wittkower has said.[2] Furthermore, these columns are twisted and spiralling upwards, carrying their intricate decorations toward the radiant Dove of God that shines on the underside of the canopy. Beyond this, as you look upward from the foot of the *Baldacchino*, the vision moves into the perfect geometrical space of Michelangelo's Renaissance dome, with its perfect circles and segments of circles, while on all four sides of the cross-over the view opens out into the semi-circular vaults of the great Church, built of course on a basically Renaissance design, according to the Renaissance ideal of perfect geometrical order, mirroring the divine harmony of all being. Thus the Baroque *Baldacchino* of Bernini must be considered within its total setting and not simply by itself, for it acts within that setting as a symbol of human aspiration, spiralling upward toward the domed and vaulted harmonies of a perfect mathematical form. Thus the Renaissance ideal of harmony controls and holds in place the violent aspirations of the Baroque spirit.

Secondly, consider the painted ceiling of the Jesuit Church in Rome, *Il Gesù*: again a basically Renaissance interior, with strict geometrical arches and a dome. But on the ceiling of the nave is a painting of the late seventeenth century which bursts out of, literally breaks through, the frame, the panel, of its Renaissance form and flows and radiates upward as though the very ceiling were opening into the heavens to reveal far off the radiant Name of Jesus. Here again, the strict Renaissance form controls and makes possible this effect of flowing Baroque aspiration.

Figure 25. Gaulli: Ceiling of *Il Gesù*, Rome. (*Photo: Alinari.*)

Figure 26. Seventeenth-century Altarpiece; Lady Chapel, Sacred Heart Church, University of Notre Dame. (*Photo: University of Notre Dame Art Gallery.*)

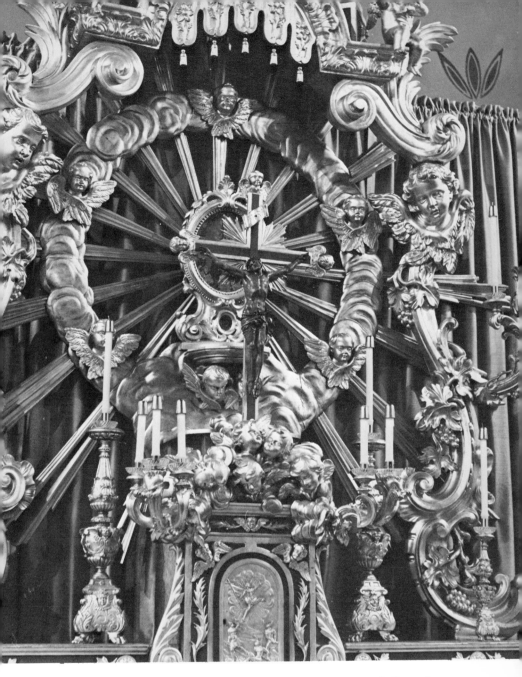

Figure 27. Seventeenth-century Altarpiece; Lady Chapel, Sacred Heart Church, University of Notre Dame: detail. (*Photo: University of Notre Dame Art Gallery.*)

Thirdly, rather unexpectedly, I would like you to think of the seventeenth-century altar-piece, said to be of the school of Bernini, that now stands at the end of the Lady Chapel at the University of Notre Dame. I have viewed it with admiration, and not only, I assure you, because it fits so well the points that I was planning to make about the Baroque. Its repeated theme of the heads and wings of cherubs, large and small, its intertwining theme of grape clusters and grape leaves, all circling richly about the center and then soaring upward in a graceful flame toward the curve of the Romanesque or Renaissance setting—all this demonstrates as well as Bernini's *Baldacchino* the way in which Baroque aspires toward and lives at its best within a geometrical harmony. But more important is the subtle firmness of the internal action: the bracing rays in the background that move out with geometrical precision from the center of that inner circle, lending a simple strength to the fragile, intricate details.

Fourthly, I would like to consider a very small, but exquisite, piece of Baroque, the wooden font-cover ascribed to Grinling Gibbons, dating from the latter part of the seventeenth century, and still in use over the font of the Church of All Hallows Barking in London. In many ways this small piece of carving illustrates perfectly the approach to the Baroque that I am trying to develop here: that the intricate repetitions and involutions and aspirations of the Baroque spirit must somehow be held under control by some kind of firm and formal setting. Thus the font-cover begins with a perfect circular block, upon which three cherubs seem to be constantly turning, moving, and aspiring upward, with the hop-plants of which the vegetative ornament is in part composed, all moving upward toward the Dove of God that forms

Figure 28. Grinling Gibbons (attrib.): limewood font-cover; Church of All Hallows Barking, London. (*Reproduced by kind permission of the Secretary-Treasurer, All Hallows Barking.*)

the peak of this triangular or conical creation. Indeed as we look closely at the sculpture we can see that it is all intricately carved within a cone. Thus Bernini's fountains live within the strict confinement of the Piazza Navona, and Juvarra's tall Church of the Superga crowns the top of its symmetrical hill outside of Turin.

Finally, inevitably, we must consider the famous sculpture of Bernini, representing the scene recorded in St. Teresa's autobiography (I quote from the translation known to Crashaw and published in 1642 under the title *The Flaming Hart*):

> I saw an Angell very neer me, towards my left side, and he appeared to me, in a Corporeall forme . . . He was not great; but rather little; yet withall, he was of very much beautie. His face was so inflamed, that he appeared to be of those most Superiour Angells, who seem to be, all in a fire; and he well might be of them, whome we call *Seraphins;* but as for me, they never tell me their names, or rankes . . . I saw, that he had a long Dart of gold in his hand; and at the end of the iron below, me thought, there was a little fire; and I conceaved, that he thrust it, some severall times, through my verie Hart, after such a manner, as that it passed the verie inwards, of my Bowells; and when he drew it back, me thought, it carried away, as much, as it had touched within me; and left all that, which remained, wholy inflamed with a great love of Almightie God.[3]

In Bernini's statuary of this vision the stone is made to flow, the robes of the Saint and the Seraph ripple as though they were water or a soft fabric, and the two figures seem to be undulating in a way that has never been seen before or since

Figure 29. Bernini: "St. Teresa in Ecstasy." Cornaro Chapel,
S. Maria della Vittoria, Rome. (*Photo: Anderson-Alinari.*)

in stone. Yet here again this dramatic image is not made to stand alone. The whole floating vision is held in focus within a highly symmetrical niche that has strict pillars on either side, while the niche itself is held in place within the whole of that enormous and dramatic composition known as the Cornaro Chapel.[4]

All this, then, by way of approach to the problem of reading Crashaw. I believe that many of the difficulties that face us in dealing with his extravagant use of Baroque techniques will disappear if we seek out and grasp the means by which these Baroque aspirations are brought into focus and under control. Let me begin with an example which has often been regarded as one of Crashaw's less successful poems: his poem entitled "The flaming Heart. Upon the booke and picture of *Teresa*. As she is usually expressed with a *Seraphim* beside her."[5] I have thought for many years that the key to this poem might well lie in discovering some particular painting of St. Teresa which Crashaw is using as the basis for this Baroque meditation. I think it may be found in a painting of St. Teresa by Crashaw's contemporary, the Antwerp artist Gerhard Seghers (see Frontispiece). This painting, now in the Museum of Fine Arts at Antwerp, was in Crashaw's day displayed in the Church of the Discalced Carmelites in Antwerp,[6] where Crashaw could have seen it during the 1640's when we know that he was living in the Low Countries. There is another copy of the painting in the English Convent at Bruges, there attributed to Velasquez, and apparently deriving from the seventeenth century.[7] The existence of this painting in two copies suggests that there may have been more copies and that perhaps this is why Crashaw thinks of the painting as representing the way in which "she is usually expressed," that is, portrayed or presented. In any case the coloration and the other characteristics of the painting fit exactly the qualities of the painting as humorously described in Crashaw's poem. With the painting before us the opening lines of the poem take on a triple reference, a characteristic flashing of Baroque wit:

> Well meaning Readers! you that come as Friends,
> And catch the pretious name this piece pretends,
> Make not so much hast to admire
> That faire cheek't fallacie of fire.

We are being addressed as readers of this particular poem, as readers, that is, interpreters, of this particular painting, and as readers of Saint Teresa's autobiography. The phrase, "the pretious name this piece pretends" (offers or sets forth), applies to all three works. Now in the opening "composition" based primarily upon the painting, the whole point lies in a witty paradox by which the poet argues that the Seraph and the Saint ought to be transposed, since the Saint is really the one who hurls the dart of Love through the means of her book. That is to say, as the Angel pierced Teresa with his dart of Love, so Teresa's book pierces us with her dart of Love. And so the poet cries with humorous exasperation:

> *Painter,* what did'st thou understand
> To put her dart into his *Hand?*
> See, even the yeares, and size of Him,
> Shew this the Mother *Seraphim.*

And, to be sure, the Seraph is a small and boyish figure compared to the larger and more mature figure of the Saint.

This is the Mistrisse *Flame*; and duteous *hee*
Her happier *fire-works*, here, comes down to see.
O most poore spirited of men!
Had thy cold Pencill kist her Pen
Thou could'st not so unkindly err
To shew us this faint shade for Her.

"Why man," the poet adds with a condescending archness:

Why man, this speakes pure mortall frame,
And mocks with Femall Frost Love's manly flame.
One would suspect thou mean'st to paint,
Some weake, inferior, *Woman Saint*.
But had thy pale-fac't purple tooke
Fire from the burning Cheekes of that *bright booke*,
Thou would'st on her have heap't up all
That could be form'd *Seraphicall*.

And it is true that the figure of Teresa in this painting has none of the ecstatic intensity of Bernini's great statue; she is a stiff and frosty figure, and the phrase "pale-fac't purple" very well describes the coloration of her face. At the same time the poet's reference to "that *bright booke*" seems to point to something in the painting itself, and indeed in the lower right-hand corner there is a bright book illuminated, as the shadow from the Cross indicates, by light that comes from the direction of the Saint's face. I suppose that the book which thus extends out toward us in space is really a Bible, but there is no lettering upon it and so the poet is free, if he wishes, to interpret this as representing one of Saint Teresa's own books. It may well be that this is why the title speaks so curiously of "the booke and picture of *Teresa*" as though they somehow occurred together in one scene. However this may be, the description of the Seraph fits exactly the quality and coloration that we see in the painting before us.

> What e're this youth of fire wore faire,
> *Rosie Fingers, Radiant Haire,*
> Glowing cheekes, and glistring wings,
> All those, faire and flagrant [i.e., burning] things,
> But before All, that fierie Dart,
> Had fill'd the *Hand* of this great *Heart.*
> Do then as equall Right requires,
> Since *his* the blushes be, and *hers* the fires,
> Resume and rectifie thy rude designe,
> Undresse thy *Seraphim* into *mine.*
> Redeeme this injury of thy art,
> Give *him* the *veyle,* give *her* the *Dart.*
> Give *him* the *veyle,* that he may cover,
> The red cheekes of a rivall'd Lover;
> Asham'd that our world now can show
> Nests of new *Seraphims* here below.
> Give *her* the *dart,* for it is *she*
> (Faire youth) shoot's both thy shafts and *thee.*

As the poet continues, line after line, to repeat this paradox in various guises, we have an elaborate example of the difference between a Baroque conceit and a metaphysical conceit. The metaphysical conceit is based upon the philosophical doctrine of correspondences[8] and it gives at its best the effect of truly exploring the nature of some metaphysical problem. But the Baroque conceit does not explore: it rather views the same paradox or symbol from various angles, reviewing and revising and restating and expanding the issue until some truth of emotion gradually grows out from all that glittering elaboration. Picking up the phrase *fire-works* from the above passage, one might say that the Baroque conceit develops like one of those seemingly unending sky-rockets which shoot out sparks of fire in a great shower, and then each spark blooms into a dozen further showers, and then all these bloom into further showers one after another after another until finally the whole display reaches its climax and the sparks fade away in the night sky. Thus at line 55 of "The flaming Heart," the first out-shooting of Love's fire reaches its climax in the rich pentameter lines that describe the effect of Teresa's book upon her readers:

> What *Magazins* of immortall armes there shine!
> Heav'ns great *Artillery* in each *Love-spun-line.*
> Give then the *Dart* to *Her,* who gives the *Flame*;
> Give *Him* the *veyle,* who kindly takes the shame.

With those lines the poem might well seem complete, as a long and witty Baroque epigram of commentary upon an interesting but imperfect painting. Crashaw has wittily taken advantage of some of the artistic techniques displayed here by this eclectic follower of Caravaggio and Rubens.[9] For Crashaw sees, no doubt, that the power of the painting resides in the Baroque quality of that Seraph who glides in with a diagonal shaft of light. The figure of the Seraph floats in mid-air, arrayed in those streaming robes of turquoise, light gold, and old rose, while the cheeks are flushed with red and the rosy fingers grip the Saint and dart. Crashaw conveniently ignores the rather effete Mannerist figure of the Angel on the other side of the picture, whose coyly posed leg reminds one

of the youth similarly posed on the left-hand side of Parmigianino's "Madonna del collo lungo."

But one never knows when a Baroque work is likely to be
finished. Crashaw looks again at the painting and decides to
take it as it is and start a new movement of thought, a movement typographically indicated in the first (1648) printing
of this poem, by having the following lines set off toward the
middle of the page:

> But if it be the frequent *Fate*
> Of worst faults to be *Fortunate*;
> If all's *prescription*; and proud wrong,
> Hearkens not to an humble song;
> For all the *Gallantry* of *Him*,
> Give me the suff'ring *Seraphim*.
> His be the bravery of all those Bright things,
> The glowing cheekes, the glittering wings,
> The *Rosie* hand, the *Radiant Dart*,
> Leave her alone the *flaming-Heart*.

It is a characteristic technique of Baroque repetition, using
the same images and phrases to begin a new approach to the
central paradox of this painting. Thus he ends the second
movement of the poem with lines that once again swell out
from the tetrameter into long pentameter lines and conclude
thus in the 1648 edition:

> *O Heart!* the equall *Poise*, of *Love's* both *Parts*,
> Big alike with *wounds* and *Darts*,
> Live in these conquering *leaves*; live all the same,
> And walke through all tongues one triumphant flame.
> Live here *great heart*; and Love, and dye, and kill,

And bleed, and wound, and yield, and conquer still.
Let this immortall Life, where e'er it comes,
Walke in a crowd of *Loves*, and *Martyrdomes*.
Let *Mystick Deaths* waite on't; and wise soules bee,
The *love-slaine-witnesses*, of this life of *Thee*.

It is a natural conclusion, returning to the book from which
the poem has drawn much of its inspiration, *The Flaming
Hart*, that is, the autobiography of Saint Teresa. And yet the
poem is not over, for when Crashaw's poems were republished
after his death, in 1652, we find a passage added, the richest
fiery shower of Baroque imagery to be found anywhere in
Crashaw's poetry, the famous lines:

O sweet incendiary! shew here thy art,
Upon this carcasse of a hard, cold, hart,
Let all thy scatter'd shafts of light, that play
Among the leaves of thy larg Books of day,
Combin'd against this *Brest* at once break in
And take away from me my self & sin,
This gratious Robbery shall thy bounty be;
And my best fortunes such fair spoiles of me.
O thou undanted daughter of desires!
By all thy dowr of *Lights* & *Fires*;
By all the eagle in thee, all the dove;
By all thy lives & deaths of love;
By thy larg draughts of intellectuall day,
And by thy thrists of love more large then they;
By all thy brim-fill'd Bowles of feirce desire
By thy last Morning's draught of liquid fire;
By the full kingdome of that finall kisse
That seiz'd thy parting Soul, & seal'd thee his;
By all the heav'ns thou hast in him
(Fair sister of the *Seraphim*!)

> By all of *Him* we have in *Thee*;
> Leave nothing of my *Self* in me.
> Let me so read thy life, that I
> Unto all life of mine may dy.

Thus the Baroque method of building, we might say, moves from the concrete to the abstract, moves from the picture before the poet's eyes to the "draughts of intellectuall day." The Baroque tries, by multiplication of sensory impressions, to exhaust the sensory and to suggest the presence of the spiritual. It does not analyze the image in Donne's manner, but rather it piles image upon image upon image, in a way that sometimes defies and destroys the basic principles of poetical architecture. Crashaw's poem "The Weeper," for example, lacks the focus of "The flaming Heart" and thus becomes only a necklace of epigrams. "The flaming Heart," however, with its sharp focus on the book and picture, develops from its rather excessively clever opening, labors for a new start in the middle, and then at the end, in the passage added in 1652, flowers triumphantly into one of the greatest passages of poetry found anywhere in the seventeenth century. As this poem shows, the Baroque work tends to be an unstable and unsteady compound, requiring for its success, in some way, the sustaining or enclosing presence of an underlying control. Crashaw's "The flaming Heart" is, I think, a barely successful work, but with the painting before our eyes it has the necessary focus and control.

One of the ways in which such control may operate to produce a more successful poem we may find in Crashaw's (presumably) earlier poem on Saint Teresa, first published in his volume of 1646. We find that control established in the first two lines of the poem, with their firm statement of the theme:

Love thou art absolute sole Lord
Of life and death, ——

We can tell from the firmness of this opening that a mature,
controlling, reasonable intelligence will be at work, dealing
with the meaning of the Saint's life, as the narrator recalls it
and recounts it for us. The poem begins with the story of the
Saint's childhood, where, as she tells, she longed to run off to
a martyrdom with the Moors:

> She never undertooke to know,
> What death with love should have to doe;
> Nor hath she e're yet understood
> Why to shew love, she should shed blood,
> Yet though she can not tell you why,
> She can *love*, and she can *dye*.

We have a tone here that resembles the smiling humor of an
adult remarking on a child's activities, and gradually the
speaker's manner becomes more and more familiar, more and
more colloquial:

> Since 'tis not to be had at home,
> Shee'l travell for *A Martyrdome*.
> No *Home* for hers confesses she,
> But where she may a Martyr be.
> Shee'l to the *Moores* and trade with them,
> For this unvalued *Diadem*,
> Shee'l offer them her dearest Breath,
> With *Christ's* name in't, in change for death.
> Shee'l bargain with them, and will give
> Them God, and teach them how to live

> In him; Or if they this deny,
> For him, she'l teach them how to dye.
> So shall she leave amongst them sown,
> Her *Lords* Blood, or at least her *own*.

He has by now adopted something like the very tone and manner of a child, and in this tone the Prologue of the poem concludes:

> Farewell then all the world! Adiew,
> *Teresa* is no more for you:
> Farewell all pleasures, sports, and joys,
> (Never till now esteemed *Toyes*)
> Farewell what ever deare may bee,
> Mother's armes or Father's Knee.
> Farewell house and farewell home:
> She's for the *Moores* and *Martyrdome*.

Then with a pause marked by an eloquent space in the edition of 1648 the speaker continues, with the adult mind reasoning in the presence of the young Saint, and foretelling her future:

> *Sweet not so fast!* Lo thy faire *Spouse*,
> Whom thou seekst with so swift vowes
> Calls thee back, and bids thee come,
> T'embrace a milder Martyrdome.

—that is, the mystic deaths of rapture and ecstacy:

> Thou art *Loves* Victim; and must dye
> A death more mysticall and *high*.

And after a series of rich images in which the dart of Cupid
is converted into the dart of the heavenly Seraph, Crashaw
moves into the erotic imagery by which the mystics of the
Church traditionally attempted to express the inexpressible:

> O how oft shalt thou complaine
> Of a sweet and subtile *paine?*
> Of intollerable *joyes?*
> Of a *death*, in which who *dyes*
> Loves his *death*, and dyes againe,
> And would for ever so be slaine!
> And lives, and dyes; and knows not why
> To live; But that he thus may never leave to dye.

But the joys that await her above are inexpressible, as he
finally concedes:

> and then,
> O what?—aske not the tongues of men.
> Angells cannot tell. Suffice,
> Thy self shall feele thine own full joyes,
> And hold them fast for ever.

Nevertheless he goes on to try to suggest those joys in heaven
by imagining how the Saint will be received there by the Virgin Mary, the Angels, and the Lord. But in all these ecstatic
visions and fiery, frequently extravagant images, the control
of the reasonable speaker runs throughout, as, in the midst of
this vision of heaven, we hear the simple language and the
terse Jonsonian couplet constantly affirming the presence of
the rational mind:

> Angells thy old friends, there shall greet thee,
> Glad at their owne home now to meet thee.
> All thy good works which went before,
> And waited for thee at the doore,
> Shall owne thee there; and all in one
> Weave a *Constellation*
> Of crownes with which the King thy spouse,
> Shall build up thy triumphant browes.
> All thy old woes shall now smile on thee,
> And thy Paines sit bright upon thee.
> All thy sorrows here shall shine,
> And thy suff'rings be divine.

And the poem concludes with the simple praise of "those waies of light,"

> Which who in death would live to see,
> Must learne in life to dye like Thee.

So in this poem the rational presence of the speaker, with his tone of familiar conversation, controls the Baroque extravaganza and makes one of Crashaw's perfect poems.

One should add, however, that these perfect poems are rather rare in the body of Crashaw's work, partly because of the very nature of the Baroque, which depends upon the daring cast of imagination for its most powerful effects, and also perhaps because Crashaw himself is living in a world of imagination that does not have its roots in England. The earlier poem on Saint Teresa achieves its success by a subtle blending of the art of Ben Jonson with the mystical fervor of Saint Teresa, but this kind of easy blending is almost unique in Crashaw's work. There is indeed very little in previous English poetry which could have prepared Crashaw to handle the Baroque mode. Robert Southwell, at the end of the sixteenth century, had made a valiant attempt to bring the Italian mode to England, in a rudimentary form. But his example was lost, as the poetical art of the Counter Reformation failed to achieve its aims in England, except as those aims were modified at the hands of Anglican poets such as George Herbert. And Herbert's modest, moderate wit creates his own version of the forms of the High Renaissance. He is not a Mannerist, he is not Baroque. Herbert in his poetry achieves the perfect harmony of a High Renaissance symbol. Yet Crashaw learned something from Herbert, the use of simple language and homely images in devotion. These he illustrates for us by an interesting poem with the following title, "On Mr. *George Herberts* booke intituled the Temple of Sacred Poems, sent to a Gentle-woman":

> Know you faire on what you looke;
> Divinest love lyes in this booke:
> Expecting fier from your eyes,
> To kindle this his sacrifice.
> When your hands untie these strings,
> Think yo'have an Angell by the wings.
> One that gladly will be nigh,
> To waite upon each morning sigh.
> To flutter in the balmy aire,
> Of your well-perfumed praier;
> These white plumes of his hee'l lend you,
> Which every day to heaven will send you:
> To take acquaintance of the *spheare*,
> And all the smooth-fac'd kindred there.

> And though *Herbert's* name doe owe
> These devotions, fairest, know
> That while I lay them on the shrine
> Of your white hand, they are mine.

Crashaw is paying tribute to Herbert in a poem composed in strict Jonsonian tetrameter couplets, while he transmutes Herbert's intimate manner of speech into another dimension, adding to it the tone of Petrarchan flattery, the tone by which the Cavalier poets conveyed their personal interest in a woman's beauty. That is, Crashaw shares these devotions with George Herbert, and yet obliquely manages to suggest that he is also devoted to this lady in a way that is somehow both religious and Cavalier. There is no poem in the works of George Herbert where he calls a woman *fairest*: he reserves that term for God.

The poem thus raises the central problem in Crashaw's aesthetic: his daring use of sensuous imagery, and especially the imagery of human love, in an effort to express his love of God, or of the Virgin Mary, or of Saint Teresa. We may see the problem clearly in a poem which Crashaw wrote in the form of an irregular Ode—a form not yet established in English literature. It is the poem entitled, "An ode which was prefixed to a Prayer booke given to a young Gentle-woman." Here Crashaw speaks to the young lady in extravagant and highly erotic images, drawing a contrast between the world of Cavalier lovers and the world of Christian lovers. The high art of prayer, he says, is not available to those who do not keep themselves pure to receive the spiritual embraces of the Virgin's Son; and so he warns her, beginning with imagery that echoes the parable of the wise and foolish Virgins (Matthew 25:1–13):

But if the noble *Bridegroome* when he come,
    Shall find the loyt'ring *Heart* from home,
        Leaving its chast aboad,
            To gad abroad,
    Amongst the gay Mates of the God of flyes;
        To take her pleasure, and to play,
        And keep the devills Holy day;
    To dance ith'sunne-shine of some smiling
                            But beguiling
    Spheare of sweet, and sugred lies,
        Some slippery paire,
        Of false perhaps as faire,
    Flattering, but forswearing eyes;

Doubtlesse some other heart
    Will get the start,
    And stepping in before,
Will take possession of the sacred store
    Of hidden sweets, and holy joyes . . .

One should notice that Crashaw here is moving far outside the range of the parable in Matthew, by developing his poem through the imagery of the popular love-songs written by Cavaliers such as Carew. Indeed, A. F. Allison has shown[10] that some of the language that follows is directly imitative of Carew's most notorious poem, his erotic piece, "A Rapture" (see the passage quoted previously in the lecture on Carew, especially the line: "From soules entranc'd in amorous languishment"). Crashaw attempts to move this highly erotic imagery up into the realm of religious mysticism, speaking of

Amorous Languishments; Luminous Trances,
Sights which are not seen with *Eyes;*

> *Spirituall*, and *Soule-piercing* glances,
> Whose pure and subtile lightning *Flyes*,
> Home to the Heart, and sets the house on fire,
> And melts it downe in sweet desire:
>
> *   *   *   *   *
>
> *Delicious deaths*, soft *exhalations*
> Of *Soule*; deare and Divine *annihilations*.
>   A thousand unknowne *Rites*
>   Of Ioyes and *rarefy'd Delights* . . .

At this point one may feel that Crashaw, with the help of St. Teresa, has transcended the physical successfully. But alas, the poem is not over. Some forty lines remain, in which Crashaw proceeds to produce a Baroque disaster, as the building collapses around a faulty metaphor:

>   Of all this store
>   Of blessings, and ten thousand more;
>   (If when he come
>   He find the Heart from home)
>   Doubtlesse he will unload
>   Himselfe some other where,
>   And powre abroad
>   His precious sweets,
>   On the faire soule whom first he meets.
>
>   *   *   *   *   *
>
> O let the blissefull *Heart* hold fast
> Her *Heav'nly Arme-full*, she shall tast,
> At once ten thousand Paradices;
>   She shall have Power,
>   To rifle and Deflower,
> The rich and Roseall spring of those rare sweets,
> Which with a swelling bosome there she meets.

It is not only that the imagery, so strongly reminiscent of Carew, leads to unfortunate associations; a more serious problem is that Crashaw is making a false effort to convey the struggle for a spiritual love in terms of the sort of rivalry that might occur between two females in their competition for an earthly lover, the sort of rivalry that Cleopatra expresses in Shakespeare's play when she sees that her handmaiden has died first, and says that she must kill herself quickly lest Iras get there first and steal the kiss from Antony:

> If she first meete the Curled *Anthony*,
> Hee'l make demand of her, and spend that kisse
> Which is my heaven to have.

But in Christian love this argument rings false because, although earthly lovers may be so exclusively attached to one woman that they have no time or love for anyone else, the love of God is boundless, and the matter of spending God's love can hardly arise. It seems a wholly unworthy argument, clever and courtly and flattering, but suggestive in a way that spoils the poem's central movement, which seems to lie in proving that heavenly joys are superior to earthly joys and not in suggesting that God may not have enough love to go round.

One may wonder what principle of art may have seemed to make it possible and acceptable to pour out such an extravaganza in honor of God. An answer may lie in a statement by Robert Southwell, who lived in Rome during the 1580's and experienced the beginnings of Baroque art as they poured forth in architecture, painting, music, and poetry. Southwell gives us, in a work published in 1591, a statement of the central principle at work in Crashaw. It occurs in a popular prose treatise that he wrote on that favorite Baroque theme: *Marie Magdalens Funeral Teares*, where he says:

> Passions I allow, and loves I approve, onely I would wishe that men would alter their object and better their intent. For passions being sequels of our nature, and allotted unto us as the handmaides of reason: there can be no doubt, but that as their author is good, and their end godly: so ther use tempered in the meane, implieth no offence.[11]

Thus the figure of the Magdalen, who washed Christ's feet with her tears and wiped them with her hair and kissed his feet and anointed them with ointment, provides a perfect symbol for the Baroque era. The goodness of the physical, "tempered in the meane," that is, reformed and rightly seen and used, constitutes the essence of the Baroque attitude, and it is this attitude that Crashaw puts to the ultimate test, sometimes failing, sometimes succeeding. Thus in his most notorious poem, "The Weeper," he piles up image upon image in honor of Mary Magdalen's penitent tears, every stanza providing its own Baroque celebration of each tear.[12] It is not so much a poem as a series of experimental epigrams, testing how far a Baroque conceit can be carried. Some stanzas succeed, some fail abominably. Thus in some Baroque churches the decoration cloys and the basic structure is lost to sight; and without a basic underlying design no work of art can hope to function. In estimating Crashaw's success, then, we must watch for the line of control. This may sometimes be found in his most extravagant odes, as, for example, in his long ode "On the name of Jesus," which, as I have shown elsewhere,[13] follows the divisions of an ancient scale of meditation, and thus proceeds by rational articulation of parts within the mind of the speaker who participates at every moment in the vision. Similarly, his other very long ode, that on the Epiphany, achieves an ultimate success by two means. First, the whole poem takes the form of an immense Baroque oratorio, sung by the Three Kings in the presence of the Christ-child and his Mother; and secondly, it derives its imagery from one basic paradox: day in night. The light shining here from the new-born Son of God is the true light, and the old Sun-god which the heathen Magi used to serve is now eclipsed. From that idea of the true light shining in darkness the whole poem develops. The sun's eclipse at the Crucifixion is taken as yet another example of the light shining in darkness. And at the close the paradox is summed up by reference to the mystical theology of the dark night of the soul, familiar to us today through its use by T. S. Eliot in his *Four Quartets*, and for Crashaw, set forth in its classic form by the writer known as Dionysius the Areopagite.

Finally, we may perhaps sum up this approach to the Baroque by looking in some detail at one of Crashaw's nearly perfect pieces: the poem "An Hymne of the Nativity, sung as by the Shepheards." It is a poem that includes the imagery of the Cavalier love song along with the tradition of the pastoral dialogue, so often sung in courtly airs and madrigals and masques. It is sung by the shepherds, sometimes singing as a choric group, and sometimes as individuals with Vergilian names, Tityrus and Thyrsis, who also sing as a duo in some stanzas. The emphasis is on the theme of love, and the basic motif is drawn from the ancient tradition of the lover's dawn-song, as represented in a poem by Carew's friend and fellow Cavalier, Sir William Davenant:

The Lark now leaves his watry Nest
   And climbing, shakes his dewy Wings;
He takes this Window for the East;
   And to implore your Light, he Sings,
Awake, awake, the Morn will never rise,
Till she can dress her Beauty at your Eies.

The Merchant bowes unto the Seamans Star,
   The Ploughman from the Sun his Season takes;
But still the Lover wonders what they are,
   Who look for day before his Mistress wakes.
Awake, awake, break through your Vailes of Lawne!
Then draw your Curtains, and begin the Dawne.

Thus in Crashaw's poem the Chorus opens by mocking the earthly sun which is now replaced by a greater light:

Come we shepheards whose blest sight
   Hath met Loves noone, in Natures night,
Come lift we up our loftier song,
   And wake the *Sun* that lyes too long.

The true light no longer comes from the earthly sun; the central image is the light that comes from the eyes of the Son of Mary; and these eyes are celebrated in the terms of the Cavalier lyric:

It was thy day, *Sweet*! and did rise,
Not from the *East*, but from thine eyes.

And the Chorus at once repeats these thematic lines. Then Thyrsis sings:

Winter chid aloud, and sent
   The angry North to wage his wars,
The North forgot his fierce intent,
   And left perfumes instead of scars,
By those sweet eyes perswasive powers,
Where he mean't frost, he scatter'd flowers.

And the Chorus repeats the last two lines. Then Tityrus and Thyrsis together sing:

We saw thee in thy Balmey Nest,
   Bright *dawn* of our eternall *day*!
We saw thine eyes break from their *East*,
   And chace the trembling shades away.
We saw thee, and we blest the sight,
We saw thee by thine owne sweet light.

And forty lines later this stanza is repeated by both shepherds word for word. In this pattern of intertwining repetitions, sometimes with a single voice, sometimes with a double voice, sometimes with a full Chorus, we have a clear example of the Baroque method of building, not by exploring images, not by analyzing them, but by piling them up one upon another until a unity, a oneness of impression is created. Here that oneness is represented in a stanza that comes near the middle of the poem:

Proud world (said I) cease your contest,
   And let the mighty *Babe* alone,
The Phaenix builds the Phaenix' nest.
   Love's Architecture is all one.

ONE HUNDRED FORTY-FOUR

In the posthumous edition of Crashaw's works the last line here is changed to read: "Love's Architecture is his own," possibly a revision made by Crashaw himself, possibly not. Whichever reading we take, the line provides a summary of Crashaw's poetical aims. Love's Architecture is all one because all nature is God's own and thus all physical nature may be included properly within the poem's building. So now we see moving toward the manger scene the snowflakes,

> Offering their whitest sheets of snow,
> To furnish the faire *Infant's* Bed:

while the Seraphim

> Their Rosie *Fleece* of *Fire* bestow,
> For well they now can spare their wings
> Since Heaven it selfe lyes here below:

and we may watch the new-born Babe reposing "his new-bloom'd *cheeke*" between his Mother's breasts:

> Sweet choice (said I!) no way but so
> Not to lye cold, yet sleep in snow.

We may do all this because the Incarnation, in Crashaw's view, has sanctified the physical, and made "all one," as the full Chorus explains in the opening stanza of the grand finale:

> Welcome all *wonders* in one sight!
> Eternitie shut in a span,
> Summer in winter, day in night,

> Heaven in Earth, and God in man;
> Great little one! Whose all embracing birth
> Lift's earth to heav'n, stoops heav'n to earth.

But the exaltation of this concept leads Crashaw then into two daring stanzas that show what a dangerous and unstable mixture the height of the Baroque may become:

> Welcom though not to gold nor silke,
> To more than *Caesars* birthright is;
> Two Sister Seas of Virgin *Milke*,
> With many a rarely temper'd Kisse
> That breath's at once both *Maide* & *Mother*,
> Warmes in the one, cooles in the other.

> She sings thy Teares a sleep, and dips
> Her Kisses in thy weeping eye,
> She spreads the red leaves of thy lips,
> That in their buds yet blushing lye.
> She 'gainst those Mother-Diamonds tries
> The points of her young Eagles eyes.

Someone, perhaps Crashaw himself, found the last of these two stanzas too much, and omitted it in the posthumous edition of 1652. These two stanzas of excess are quickly brought under control in the remainder of the poem, where Crashaw gracefully concludes with stanzas that express the love of God with all the art of the Cavalier, mingling pastoral and Petrarchan themes with the imagery of divine love:

> Yet when young *Aprill's* husband showers,
> Shall blesse the fruitfull *Maia's* bed,
> Wee'l bring the first borne of her flowers,

To kisse thy feet, and crowne thy head.
To thee dread *Lamb*! whose love must keepe
The shepheards more than they their sheepe.

To thee meeke *Majestie*! soft King
   Of simple *Graces* and sweet *Loves*;
Each of us his *Lamb* will bring,
   Each his paire of Silver Doves,
Till burnt at last in fire of thy faire eyes,
Our selves become our owne best sacrifice.

IV

Andrew Marvell

The Mind's Happiness

Figure 30. Andrew Marvell: artist unknown. (*National Portrait Gallery, London; reproduced by kind permission of the Trustees of the National Portrait Gallery.*)

". . . he was also a typical and unmistakable mannerist by reason of what he betrays about himself and those whose portraits he paints, as well as by what he holds back and conceals behind the cold and severe expressions, the self-discipline that his sitters preserve in relation to the outside world, the 'armour of cool bearing' with which he protects them against the importunity of the inquisitive." (Hauser, *Mannerism*, I, 199; referring to Bronzino.)

IV

Andrew Marvell

The Mind's Happiness

Thomas Carew and George Herbert were almost exact contemporaries, members of the generation immediately following the great masters, Donne and Jonson; and both Carew and Herbert were, in their own ways, courtly poets, gathering up in their collected poems all the grace and wit of the world of song that made this era of English culture the greatest era of English music. Both were, in their own ways, courtiers: one, the courtier of the Queen of Love and Beauty, the earthly Venus; and the other, the courtier of Heavenly Love, addressing to his Lord the art that the Cavalier world addressed to Mortal Love. Both sang their songs in what they felt to be a realm of true security: Carew within the elegant Court of Charles I, and Herbert within the "perfect lineaments" of "The British Church":

> A fine aspect in fit aray,
> Neither too mean, nor yet too gay,

Shows who is best.
Outlandish looks may not compare:
For all they either painted are,
Or else undrest.

. . . . .

But, dearest Mother, what those misse,
The mean, thy praise and glorie is,
And long may be.
Blessed be God, whose love it was
To double-moat thee with his grace,
And none but thee.

Richard Crashaw and Andrew Marvell, in the next generation, knew very little of such security, since both lived through the era of those Civil Wars which shattered the established institutions of Church and State. For a time, during the 1630's, they shared a brief security in place and thought, at Cambridge University, where Marvell was a student at Trinity, and Crashaw, older by about nine years, lived down the road a bit as a fellow of Peterhouse. In 1637 their poems (in Latin and Greek) appeared together in a volume published at Cambridge honoring the birth of the Princess Anne. At this time both poets seem to have shared High Church tendencies: Marvell seems for a short time to have been converted to the Roman Catholic faith, as Crashaw was to be a few years later. But during the Civil Wars their ways utterly diverged. Crashaw, ousted from his post at Peterhouse because of his loyalty to King and Church, went abroad, embraced the Roman faith, and died at the shrine of Loreto in the same year that saw his King's death, in 1649. Marvell, after a period of mixed loyalties, mirrored in the ambiguities of his famous

"Horatian Ode," at last gave his full support to the cause of the Commonwealth and, in particular, to Oliver Cromwell. Both the personal and the poetical careers of Crashaw and of Marvell may be taken to symbolize two utterly different ways of resolving the fierce dilemmas of the day.

In this hiatus, a period when a new world of religious and political thought was in the process of violent formation, Marvell looks back upon the remains of courtly culture with attraction and regret, as we may see from the poem that he wrote "To his Noble Friend Mr. Richard Lovelace, upon his Poems"—a poem prefaced to Lovelace's volume of Cavalier poetry published in 1649:

> Our times are much degenerate from those
> Which your sweet Muse which your fair Fortune chose,
> And as complexions alter with the Climes,
> Our wits have drawne th'infection of our times.
> That candid Age no other way could tell
> To be ingenious, but by speaking well.
> Who best could prayse, had then the greatest prayse,
> Twas more esteemd to give, then weare the Bayes:
> Modest ambition studi'd only then,
> To honour not her selfe, but worthy men.
> These vertues now are banisht out of Towne,
> Our Civill Wars have lost the Civicke crowne.
> He highest builds, who with most Art destroys,
> And against others Fame his owne employs.
> I see the envious Caterpillar sit
> On the faire blossome of each growing wit.[1]

It is appropriate that Marvell should thus pay tribute to this poet, whose songs to Lucasta and to Althea represent the very essence of the Cavalier devotion to the Lady and to the King, expressed with all the art of courtly elegance. I say it is appropriate, because Marvell's poetry in many ways derives from the Mannerist art that we have seen in Carew and his fellow Cavaliers. Marvell has a love song, "The Match," addressed to a girl named Celia, praising her as Nature's treasury of *"Orientest* Colours," "Essences most pure," and "sweetest Perfumes." He has another song addressed to a fair Lady singing—one of Carew's favorite themes. He has of course that famous poem "To his Coy Mistress," following in the tradition represented by Carew's poem in the same meter: "To A. L. Perswasions to love." And he has three graceful pastoral dialogues where nymph and shepherd converse in singing repartee, as in two elegant songs by Carew. In many ways Marvell and Carew show the same inheritance of the European love-lyric, modified by an infusion of Donne's argumentative wit, and by Jonson's art of terse craftsmanship.

Yet at the same time Marvell inherits the tradition of the religious love-lyric brought to perfection by Herbert, and in his poem "The Coronet" we find him "Dismantling all the fragrant Towers" which he has used to adorn his shepherdess's head, in an effort to recreate the flowers of secular poetry as a tribute to his Savior. But he finds the serpent old entwined within his garland of devotion, for motives of fame and self-interest have made the attempted tribute impure; and so he prays:

> But thou who only could'st the Serpent tame,
> Either his slipp'ry knots at once untie,
> And disintangle all his winding Snare:
> Or shatter too with him my curious frame:

And let these wither, so that he may die,
Though set with Skill and chosen out with Care.
That they, while Thou on both their Spoils dost tread,
May crown thy Feet, that could not crown thy Head.

It is, for the most part, a powerful effort in the devotional
mode of Herbert, and yet in the last few lines the gnarled and
intricate evolution of thought, with a tortured vagueness in
the pronouns, creates an effect quite different from the characteristic serenity of Herbert's endings. We need to remember
such conclusions in Herbert as these:

> Love is that liquour sweet and most divine,
> Which my God feels as bloud; but I, as wine.
>
> *   *   *   *   *
>
> But while I bustled, I might heare a friend
> Whisper, *How wide is all this long pretence!*
> *There is in love a sweetnesse readie penn'd:*
> *Copie out onely that, and save expense.*
>
> *   *   *   *   *
>
> But grones are quick, and full of wings,
> And all their motions upward be;
> And ever as they mount, like larks they sing;
> The note is sad, yet musick for a King.
>
> *   *   *   *   *
>
> But as I rav'd and grew more fierce and wilde
> At every word,
> Me thoughts I heard one calling, *Child*!
> And I reply'd, *My Lord*.
>
> *   *   *   *   *
>
> You must sit down, sayes Love, and taste my meat:
> So I did sit and eat.

Far from achieving the goal of humility that Herbert implies in those endings, Marvell ends with an intricate flourish of wit that shows the pride of an indomitable intellect, saying in effect, "I pray all this in order that my poems, while you, God, tread both on Satan and on my poetry, may crown your feet, since they could not succeed in crowning your head." It is all too clever, and yet the whole ending functions in the poem to show that Marvell's Mannerist pride in his exquisite contrivance, his "curious frame," is still a part of his being.

So in Marvell the art of the Cavalier and the religious problems of the time converge in an uneasy alliance: set with skill, and chosen out with care, his poems contemplate, from various angles, the deepest issues of the age. We can feel these issues breaking through the fragile Mannerist artifact in one of his pastoral dialogues, entitled "Clorinda and Damon," where the pagan world of "Gather ye rosebuds" meets with the Christian sense of mortality and sin.[2] Clorinda, the shepherdess, invites Damon to come to her grassy meadow "Where *Flora* blazons all her pride." "The Grass I aim to feast thy Sheep," she explains, "The Flow'rs I for thy Temples keep." But Damon refuses, saying "Grass withers; and the Flow'rs too fade." But Clorinda insists upon her *carpe diem* theme, and so their interplay continues:

> C. Seize the short Joyes then, ere they vade.
>   Seest thou that unfrequented Cave?
> D. That den? C. Loves Shrine. D. But Virtue's Grave.
> C. In whose cool bosome we may lye
>   Safe from the Sun. D. not Heaven's Eye.
> C. Near this, a Fountaines liquid Bell
>   Tinkles within the concave Shell.

> D. Might a Soul bath there and be clean,
>   Or slake its Drought?   C. What is't you mean?

Clearly Damon has at last shattered Clorinda's complacency and has indeed shattered the pastoral scene with the fearful religious question. And Damon then goes on to explain how all is now changed for him, alluding to Christ under the conventional name of Pan, as in Milton's "Nativity Ode":

> D. These once had been enticing things,
>   *Clorinda*, Pastures, Caves, and Springs.
> C. And what late change?   D. The other day
>   *Pan* met me.   C. What did great *Pan* say?
> D. Words that transcend poor Shepherds skill,
>   But He ere since my Songs does fill:
>   And his Name swells my slender Oate.
> C. Sweet must *Pan* sound in *Damons* Note.
> D. *Clorinda's* voice might make it sweet.
> C. Who would not in *Pan's* Praises meet?
>
>   Chorus.
>   Of *Pan* the flowry Pastures sing,
>   Caves eccho, and the Fountains ring.
>   Sing then while he doth us inspire;
>   For all the World is our *Pan's* Quire.

It is a happy reconciliation, but does Clorinda know what Damon means by Pan? Or does Damon know what Clorinda means by Pan? Is not this happy Chorus perhaps a mixed marriage of voices singing different gods? They are too much in love, it seems, to inquire exactly what each of them means by Pan. Here, within the poem's fragile artifice, the clash between Christian and Pagan threatens for a moment the

THE WIT OF LOVE

destruction of both the Mannerist and the pastoral world; but the conflict is gaily and humorously healed.

A more dangerous threat is perhaps suggested in the "Dialogue between Thyrsis and Dorinda," where the shepherd Thyrsis describes his pastoral Elizium in such attractive terms that the naive nymph Dorinda suddenly falls sick of longing for it and suggests that they commit suicide in order to achieve such beauty in the after-life:

Dorinda. Ah me, ah me. (*Thyrsis.*) *Dorinda,* why do'st Cry?

Dorinda. I'm sick, I'm sick, and fain would dye:
Convince me now, that this is true;
By bidding, with mee, all adieu.

Thyrsis. I cannot live, without thee, I
Will for thee, much more with thee dye.

Chorus. Then let us give *Carillo* charge o'th Sheep,
And thou and I'le pick poppies and them steep
In wine, and drink on't even till we weep,
So shall we smoothly pass away in sleep.

Is Marvell suggesting that there may be a certain danger in the tendency of some religious sects to emphasize the joys of the future life? It would be going too far to say this: one might better say only that Marvell's curiously detached mind is here using the pastoral artifice to contemplate, at a considerable distance, a possible religious issue. This indeed might be said of all five of the poems of conflict that Marvell has cast into the dialogue form, poems that range from the purely spiritual to the purely carnal: from the spiritual victory of the Resolved Soul to the physical victory of the girl Thestylis, as she entices Ametas into her hay-mow, with the words:

ONE HUNDRED FIFTY-EIGHT

> What you cannot constant hope
> Must be taken as you may.

And Ametas answers:

> Then let's both lay by our Rope,
> And go kiss within the Hay.

Even when the pastoral guard is dropped and the religious issues are joined head-on, one senses the curious detachment of Marvell's wit—curious in our meaning of the word and also in Marvell's own meaning of "exquisite," "elegant." Consider the poem that opens Marvell's collected poems of 1681, "A Dialogue between the Resolved Soul, and Created Pleasure," where Marvell deals with a central topic of the age, "the spiritual combat." The poem opens traditionally enough, with a familiar self-address, echoing the words of St. Paul in the Epistle to the Ephesians:

> Courage my Soul, now learn to wield
> The weight of thine immortal Shield.
> Close on thy Head thy Helmet bright.
> Ballance thy Sword against the Fight.

But as we read on we may wonder exactly what is happening, for the temptations of Pleasure seem so absurdly over-drawn:

> On these downy Pillows lye,
> Whose soft Plumes will thither fly:
> On these Roses strow'd so plain
> Lest one Leaf thy Side should strain.

And the Soul's answers seem so clipped and pat and almost smug:

My gentler Rest is on a Thought,
Conscious of doing what I ought.

* * * * *

A Soul that knowes not to presume
Is Heaven's and its own perfume.

So the whole poem comes to suggest an undercurrent of playful wit, reinforced and brought into the open by the Soul's pun on the word *Chordage* in answer to the temptation by the pleasure of music:

Cease Tempter. None can chain a mind
Whom this sweet Chordage cannot bind.

Is the poem a serious exercise in self-analysis, or is it rather a graceful exercise of lyric wit in the Jonsonian mode of terse craftsmanship?

So it is too with "A Dialogue between the Soul and Body," where Marvell seems to enjoy developing the ingenious play of wit by which Soul and Body, each speaking in monologue rather than dialogue, blindly denounce each other for causing each other's torment. Then the poet at the close cleverly suggests a resolution to the dilemma by adding four lines to the Body's stanza:

What but a Soul could have the wit
To build me up for Sin so fit?
So Architects do square and hew,
Green Trees that in the Forest grew.

So Marvell suggests to us, perhaps, that there is some purpose in this conflict that the two antagonists do not grasp—that there is a higher architecture in which both Soul and Body are made according to the Architect's design.

This range of subject is characteristic of Marvell's lyric poetry, which ranges from the total celebration of the Soul in "On a Drop of Dew," to the total celebration of the claims of physical passion in "To his Coy Mistress." I say *total*. And yet both poems are written with their own kind of curious detachment. The poem "On a Drop of Dew" is a perfectly executed spiritual exercise. It presents first a clear visual image or similitude (a composition of place): the drop of dew lying on the purple flower; then the understanding proceeds to apply this image to the plight of the human Soul; and finally the power of the will draws forth a firm spiritual meaning. Thus the middle of the poem develops an Augustinian theme:

> So the Soul, that Drop, that Ray
> Of the clear Fountain of Eternal Day,
> Could it within the humane flow'r be seen,
> Remembring still its former height,
> Shuns the sweat leaves and blossoms green;
> And, recollecting its own Light,
> Does, in its pure and circling thoughts, express
> The greater Heaven in an Heaven less.

The word *recollecting* means not only "remembering," and "collecting together," or "concentrating the attention," but it also suggests the spiritual state of "recollection," in which the Soul is absorbed in religious contemplation, leading to the state of "illumination." It would seem that Marvell is tending toward an intense insight, reminiscent of the poetry of Henry Vaughan. But then the poem breaks away into a strange and unexpected dance: a neat series of lines paced with a Cavalier elegance:

> In how coy a Figure wound,
> Every way it turns away:
> So the World excluding round,
> Yet receiving in the Day.
> Dark beneath, but bright above:
> Here disdaining, there in Love,
> How loose and easie hence to go:
> How girt and ready to ascend.
> Moving but on a point below,
> It all about does upwards bend.
> Such did the Manna's sacred Dew destil;
> White, and intire, though congeal'd and chill.
> Congeal'd on Earth: but does, dissolving, run
> Into the Glories of th' Almighty Sun.

It is a perfect spiritual exercise—yes—but may one say that it is almost too perfect, too coolly contrived to create a deep religious feeling? The fact that Marvell also wrote a companion poem to this in Latin, using the same themes and images, may suggest the highly tentative, detached, and experimental nature of the approach to religious experience that Marvell is dealing with here. The Latin poem and the English poem work together to create the impression that this poet is contemplating here the possibility of engaging in religious contemplation, but has not re-created the experience of contemplation itself.

This poem, in its ebbing and flowing lines, suggests a cool and miniature version of one of Crashaw's passionate Odes or abundant Hymns, and indeed in one phrase, "its own Tear," the poem echoes a phrase used in Crashaw's poem to Mary Magdalene entitled "The Teare." One may fairly grasp the curiously detached and guarded quality of Marvell's religious poems by contrasting the Baroque exuberance of Crashaw's poems on the tears of the Magdalene with the cool and logical precision of Marvell's contribution to this literature of penitence—his poem "Eyes and Tears." Two stanzas from Crashaw's "The Weeper" will serve to make the point, if set against the opening and closing stanzas of Marvell's poem:

> 15 O cheekes! Beds of chast loves,
> By your own showers seasonably dash't,
>   Eyes! nests of milkie Doves
> In your owne wells decently washt.
> O wit of love that thus could place,
> Fountaine and Garden in one face!

> 18 'Twas his well pointed dart
> That dig'd these wells, and drest this Vine,
>   And taught that wounded heart,
> The way into those weeping Eyne,
> Vaine loves avant! Bold hands forbeare,
> The Lamb hath dipt his white foote here.

Now contrast these exuberant stanzas by Crashaw with the lucid, logical couplets of Marvell:

I.

How wisely Nature did decree,
With the same Eyes to weep and see!
That, having view'd the object vain,
They might be ready to complain.

II.

And, since the Self-deluding Sight,
In a false Angle takes each hight;
These Tears which better measure all,
Like wat'ry Lines and Plummets fall.

XII.

Ope then mine Eyes your double Sluice,
And practise so your noblest Use.
For others too can see, or sleep;
But only humane Eyes can weep.

XIII.

Now like two Clouds dissolving, drop,
And at each Tear in distance stop:
Now like two Fountains trickle down:
Now like two floods o'return and drown.

XIIII.

Thus let your Streams o'reflow your Springs,
Till Eyes and Tears be the same things:
And each the other's difference bears;
These weeping Eyes, those seeing Tears.

One may wonder whether this is a religious poem, or whether it is better called a witty Mannerist exercise on a religious theme, mingling cleverly the argued wit of Donne, the Baroque paradoxes of Crashaw, and the neat trim craftsmanship of Jonson. However this may be, the strict rational discipline of the poem seems ill suited to the far-flung nature of the imagery here, with the result that the images have an effect of being coolly contrived, not growing out of some inevitable problem or passion, as in the better poems of Donne or Crashaw.

We can see somewhat the same effect in Marvell's poem "The Definition of Love," where Marvell seems determined to outdo Donne in the ingenuity of his metaphysical conceits. It is Marvell's most Donne-like poem, and yet the effect of these terse, clipped, neat stanzas is ultimately quite unlike Donne.

I.

My Love is of a birth as rare
As 'tis for object strange and high:
It was begotten by despair
Upon Impossibility.

II.

Magnanimous Despair alone
Could show me so divine a thing,
Where feeble Hope could ne'r have flown
But vainly flapt its Tinsel Wing.

III.

And yet I quickly might arrive
Where my extended Soul is fixt,
But Fate does Iron wedges drive,
And alwaies crouds it self betwixt.

IV.

For Fate with jealous Eye does see
Two perfect Loves; nor lets them close:

Their union would her ruine be,
And her Tyrannick pow'r depose.

V.

And therefore her Decrees of Steel
Us as the distant Poles have plac'd,
(Though Loves whole World on us doth wheel)
Not by themselves to be embrac'd.

It has surely a measure of Donne's passionate reasoning in his pursuit of Love's philosophy, but the reasoning here is so coolly and deliberately done that the passion is carefully tamped down, and never threatens to escape as it so often does in Donne's anguish. So Marvell's "Definition" firmly ends:

VII.

As Lines so Loves *oblique* may well
Themselves in every Angle greet:
But ours so truly *Paralel*,
Though infinite can never meet.

VIII.

Therefore the Love which us doth bind,
But Fate so enviously debarrs,
Is the Conjunction of the Mind,
And Opposition of the Stars.

We remember how in Donne's "Valediction: forbidding Mourning," the geometrical conceit at the close had served as an expression of the strain and anguish that besets the parting of two true lovers, to whom separation is as a death. But here, although one admires the geometrical neatness of this conclusion, there is little sense of an underlying passion. Here again Marvell seems to be contemplating the feeling of what it might be like to be in love instead of creating the dramatic state of Love's actuality.

Even the famous "To his Coy Mistress" has, in its own way, a quality of detachment about it, for all its apparent urgency. We may feel this quality with particular force if we compare the poem with Robert Herrick's "Corinna's Going A-Maying." In Herrick's poem human love is represented as a part of the fruitful process of nature: love blooms and dies as nature dies, and the emphasis falls upon the beauty of the natural process. Herrick's poem is in tune with nature, but Marvell's poem is at war with nature; the speaker's wit seems to resent the shortness of life, which Herrick's poem sadly accepts. The speaker's tone toward his reserved and respectable young Lady shifts within each of the poem's three sections, moving from sly, humorous banter, to sardonic threats, and finally to something like a fierce desperation. The poem opens with mock politeness:

> Had we but World enough, and Time,
> This coyness Lady were no crime.
> We would sit down, and think which way
> To walk, and pass our long Loves Day.
> Thou by the *Indian Ganges* side
> Should'st Rubies find: I by the Tide
> Of *Humber* would complain.

For, Lady, he says, "you deserve this State," this pomp, this ceremony, "Nor would I love at lower rate," that is, lower estimation. But, he continues, we have very little time:

> And yonder all before us lye
> Desarts of vast Eternity.

ONE HUNDRED SIXTY-SEVEN

And after a gruesome reminder of what the worms will do
to her he ends with a sardonic tone of excessive politeness:

> The Grave's a fine and private place,
> But none I think do there embrace.

And then he swings quickly into his conclusion with inevitable
logic:

> Now therefore, while the youthful hew
> Sits on thy skin like morning glew, . . .

(I keep the reading of the first edition instead of using the
common emendation "dew," because it seems likely that
"glew" is simply a variant spelling of the word "glow," and
that what the poet is saying here is that the youthful color
sitting on her skin is like the morning-glow of sunrise.)[3]

> And while thy willing Soul transpires
> At every pore with instant Fires,
> Now let us sport us while we may;
> And now, like am'rous birds of prey,
> Rather at once our Time devour,
> Than languish in his slow-chapt pow'r.
> Let us roll all our Strength, and all
> Our sweetness, up into one Ball:
> And tear our Pleasures with rough strife,
> Thorough the Iron gates of Life.
> Thus, though we cannot make our Sun
> Stand still, yet we will make him run.

"We cannot make our Sun/Stand still," like Joshua or like
Zeus when he seduced Alcmene and produced Heracles, but

we can at least eat up our time with devouring strife. But what kind of pleasure is this? Marvell has consumed all the natural beauty out of the experience of human love. Is he suggesting that perhaps the rosebud-philosophy is self-destructive, corrosive, and ultimately empty? Is this a love poem at all? Is it not rather a poem about man's fear of Time?

I hope my emphasis on Marvell's detachment, his concern for style, his coolly crafted art, has not served to suggest that I think Marvell's poems are themselves rather empty. This is the problem that one often faces in dealing with Mannerist art. Is the manner mere imitation, lacking any depth or real significance, or is the manner a way of guarding the mind's uncertainty in its quest for ultimate values? Does the elegance of style stand as a mask before some inner tension? Or does it serve as a defense against the revelation of some intimate, impossible ideal? In asking this question I am moving away from the earlier and simpler account of Mannerism that I used in discussing the poetry of Carew. I am moving away from John Shearman's emphasis on *style* as the prime criterion, and moving on into the deeper and more inclusive account of Mannerism set forth in the splendid study of Arnold Hauser.[4] The greatness of Hauser's conception of Mannerism lies in the fact that he can include the spiritual, the intellectual, the playful, the poignant, and the elegant all within one compelling account of a great artistic movement, for which, I am convinced, Andrew Marvell stands as a prime English representative. For Marvell has the qualities that Hauser finds at the heart of Mannerism. "A certain piquancy, a predilection for the subtle, the strange, the over-strained, the abstruse and yet stimulating, the pungent, the bold, and the challenging, are characteristic of mannerist art in all its phases," says Hauser. And he adds, "It is often this piquancy —a playful or compulsive deviation from the normal, an affected, frisky quality, or a tormented grimace—that first betrays the mannerist nature of a work. The virtuosity that is always displayed contributes greatly to this piquancy."[5] But underneath this playfulness or piquancy Hauser finds a quality that seems to me to lie at the very center of Marvell's vision: an intellectualized view of existence that makes it possible to maintain all the conflicting elements of life within a flexible yet highly regulated vision:

> The conflict expresses the conflict of life itself and the ambivalence of all human attitudes; in short, it expresses the dialectical principle that underlies the whole of the mannerist outlook. This is based, not merely on the conflicting nature of occasional experience, but on the permanent ambiguity of all things, great and small, and on the impossibility of attaining certainty about anything. All the products of the mind must therefore show that we live in a world of irreducible tensions and mutually exclusive and yet inter-connected opposites. For nothing in this world exists absolutely, the opposite of every reality is also real and true. Everything is expressed in extremes opposed to other extremes, and it is only by this paradoxical pairing of opposites that meaningful statement is possible. This paradoxical approach does not signify, however, that each statement is the retraction of the last, but that truth inherently has two sides, that reality is Janus-faced, and that adherence to truth and reality involves the avoidance of all over-simplification and comprehending things in their complexity.[6]

Thus Marvell, in 1650, could write that great "Horatian Ode" in which he carefully weighs the virtues of the King and of Cromwell, seeing the poignancy of one and the power of the other, including both within an intellectual vision that is able to choose, at the end, the side of destiny, without ceasing to regret the necessity of the destruction of ancient institutions. And alongside the paradoxical vision of that Ode, Marvell could then place, perhaps only a few years later, his great poem "The Garden," in which the joys of intellectual peace are praised as the center of existence. Thus, in the famous central stanzas of "The Garden," the speaker finds his harmony, both physical and mental, in an easy relationship with the created universe:

> What wond'rous Life in this I lead!
> Ripe Apples drop about my head;
> The Luscious Clusters of the Vine
> Upon my Mouth do crush their Wine;
> The Nectaren, and curious Peach,
> Into my hands themselves do reach;
> Stumbling on Melons, as I pass,
> Insnar'd with Flow'rs, I fall on Grass.

And while the body enjoys that fortunate fall, the mind, withdrawing from these lesser (physical) pleasures, discovers and creates its own happiness:

> Mean while the Mind, from pleasure less,
> Withdraws into its happiness:
> The Mind, that Ocean where each kind
> Does streight its own resemblance find;

> Yet it creates, transcending these,
> Far other Worlds, and other Seas;
> Annihilating all that's made
> To a green Thought in a green Shade.

The mind, that is to say, contains within itself the images drawn from the outer world; yet it creates, transcending these, worlds of the human imagination, which arise from the creative and unifying power that Marvell suggests in the word *annihilating*. There is an allusion here to the mystical usage of the word, as Crashaw has used it when he speaks of "soft *exhalations*/Of *Soule;* deare and Divine *annihilations*."[7] But of course the word is used by Marvell in a characteristically playful sense, for in mystical annihilation all sensory images are destroyed and the soul ascends into the realm of pure spirit. In "The Garden" the process of annihilation blends the greenness of nature with the abstract purity of thought. And even as the soul ascends upward in Marvell's poem, thought remains still allied with sensory things, as we may see from the next stanza, where the soul does not leave the physical, but remains connected with the body through the tree:

> Here at the Fountains sliding foot,
> Or at some Fruit-trees mossy root,
> Casting the Bodies Vest aside,
> My Soul into the boughs does glide:
> There like a Bird it sits, and sings,
> Then whets, and combs its silver Wings;
> And, till prepar'd for longer flight,
> Waves in its Plumes the various Light.

Then in the next stanza Marvell's quiet humor reminds us that the mind is still within the world of man, as he humor-

ously recalls Adam's happy state, before Eve, the cause of all
his woes, was created as an help meet for him:

> Such was that happy Garden-state,
> While Man there walk'd without a Mate:
> After a Place so pure, and sweet,
> What other Help could yet be meet!
> But 'twas beyond a Mortal's share
> To wander solitary there:
> Two Paradises 'twere in one
> To live in Paradise alone.

And finally, in Stanza IX, perhaps a symbol of numerical perfection, Marvell returns gently and easily into the world of
time as he presents his image of the floral sun-dial, and
concludes:

> How could such sweet and wholsome Hours
> Be reckon'd but with herbs and flow'rs!

Less wholesome hours, no doubt, await the speaker in the
outer world, but the mind's happiness remains within, a sure
retreat that underlies the varied explorations conveyed in all
his other poems.

As at the end of a long avenue, one catches a distant glimpse
of this ideal in the poem that might be regarded as the most
obviously Mannerist of all Marvell's works, the one entitled
"The Gallery," which Jean Hagstrum has suggested[8] must
be influenced by the famous volume of Marino's poetry entitled *La Galeria*, where Marino bases his poetry upon various
paintings and sculptures, or gives in similar terms imaginary
portraits of his own. Following this mode of action Marvell

here presents to us the art gallery of his soul, hung, he says, with various portraits of his Lady:

> *Clora* come view my Soul, and tell
> Whether I have contriv'd it well.

It opens with the characteristic gesture of all Mannerist art: he urges the viewer to watch closely and to judge whether the work is well "contrived." Here in his Soul, he says, she is first painted in the dress "Of an Inhumane Murtheress," tormenting her lover with "Black Eyes, red Lips, and curled Hair." Then on the other side he says she is drawn as a great Renaissance nude:

> Like to *Aurora* in the Dawn;
> When in the East she slumb'ring lyes,
> And stretches out her milky Thighs;

In the next painting she is shown as an "Enchantress," and in the next she sits afloat "Like *Venus* in her pearly Boat," as in some painting by a Botticelli. "These Pictures and a thousand more," he says, form in his Soul "a Collection choicer far/Then or *White-hall's*, or *Mantua's* were." That is to say, choicer than King Charles's collection in his palace at Whitehall, or the collection of the Duke of Mantua which Charles had purchased. Then he concludes with a significant movement of the mind toward a scene that forms the deep and inner center of all Marvell's poetry, in the close revealing the ideal that underlies his art:

> But, of these Pictures and the rest,
> That at the Entrance likes me best:

Where the same Posture, and the Look
Remains, with which I first was took.
A tender Shepherdess, whose Hair
Hangs loosely playing in the Air,
Transplanting Flow'rs from the green Hill,
To crown her Head, and Bosome fill.

The memory of the green hill, the pastoral landscape, the effort to regain the vision of a lost garden—this is the deep theme of Marvell's poetry, the center of security which lies within his mannered, stylish surface, which is in fact guarded and treasured within that surface. Here Marvell joins the central quest of many of the most significant writers of this mid-century era of turmoil. On the one side he joins the pagan Paradise of Robert Herrick, with the many "fresh and fragrant" girls that live like flowers and live with flowers throughout the *Hesperides*. And on the other side he joins Henry Vaughan, Thomas Traherne, and John Milton in *Paradise Lost*—all in their own ways keeping a kindred image of a pastoral Paradise before their inner eyes.[9] And other writers too, notably Izaak Walton, in his *Compleat Angler*, where he gives us a georgic pastoral,[10] in which the art of fishing provides the setting for a truly religious retreat into an inner Paradise, where man is at one with Nature and with God.

The meaning of this central quest of the mid-century may be suggested in Marvell's small poem "Bermudas," where the longing for the earthly Paradise represents a search for peace amidst the cruel controversies of the age, the ravaging of England by the Civil Wars, the efforts at repressive persecution by whichever side was temporarily dominant in the religious conflicts of the day. Here we have the imagined song of the Puritan refugees from King Charles's High Church policy, refugees who found peace in the remote Bermudas, as others did in Massachusetts:

> What should we do but sing his Praise
> That led us through the watry Maze,
> Unto an Isle so long unknown,
> And yet far kinder than our own?
> Where he the huge Sea-Monsters wracks,
> That lift the Deep upon their Backs.
> He lands us on a grassy Stage;
> Safe from the Storms, and Prelat's rage.
> He gave us this eternal Spring,
> Which here enamells every thing;
> And sends the Fowl's to us in care,
> On daily Visits through the Air.
> He hangs in shades the Orange bright,
> Like golden Lamps in a green Night.
>
> * * * * *
>
> And in these Rocks for us did frame
> A Temple, where to sound his Name.
> Oh let our Voice his Praise exalt,
> Till it arrive at Heavens Vault:

It is a Puritan Psalm of Thanksgiving in praise of the Creator's bounty and goodness, by which they have been enabled to reach a place amid these remote rocks to praise their Lord. One should note that, as in *Paradise Lost*, the meaning of Paradise lies in the human response to nature and not in the beauties of nature itself. The physical imagery of nature's beauty is meaningless unless man lives in a state of joyful harmony, with gratitude toward the Creator. Or rather one might say that outer nature has no beauty except as man receives it gratefully within the mind.

Such an attitude toward the meaning of Eden we may see developed in Marvell's symbol of the Mower, whose pastoral existence has been destroyed by love of his particular Eve, named Juliana. In "The Mower to the Glo-Worms" we see that these beneficent works of nature now shine in vain,

> Since *Juliana* here is come,
> For She my Mind hath so displac'd
> That I shall never find my home.

And he continues in "The Mower's Song":

> My Mind was once the true survey
> Of all these Medows fresh and gay:
> And in the greenness of the Grass
> Did see its Hopes as in a Glass;
> When *Juliana* came, and She
> What I do to the Grass, does to my Thoughts and Me.

But now he reproaches the meadows for growing in luxuriance when he is pining away with frustrated love. They ought, he feels, to be fading away like him, but they have instead disloyally forsaken him and have gone their own way. The pastoral condition, we see, depends upon man's state of mind:[11] it is by this that nature becomes either a Paradise or a ruin. Externally, the Mower as he mows is simply doing his usual job: to reap crops, to clear the land for further crops. This is his natural function. But now his function is perverted by sorrow and pain: and so in "Damon the Mower" he

sees nature falsely and recklessly seeks revenge upon it for a
state of mind which creates his own fall and ruin:

> While thus he threw his Elbow round,
> Depopulating all the Ground,
> And, with his whistling Sythe, does cut
> Each stroke between the Earth and Root,
> The edged Stele by careless chance
> Did into his own Ankle glance;
> And there among the Grass fell down,
> By his own Sythe, the Mower mown.

But his own self-destruction is only a symbol of man's
general corruption of these natural harmonies, as the Mower
declares in his tirade against artificial gardens:

> Luxurious Man, to bring his Vice in use,
>   Did after him the World seduce:
> And from the fields the Flow'rs and Plants allure,
>   Where Nature was most plain and pure.
> He first enclos'd within the Gardens square
>   A dead and standing pool of Air:
> And a more luscious Earth for them did knead,
>   Which stupifi'd them while it fed.
>
>   *   *   *   *   *
>
> 'Tis all enforc'd; the Fountain and the Grot;
>   While the sweet Fields do lye forgot:
> Where willing Nature does to all dispence
>   A wild and fragrant Innocence:
> And *Fauns* and *Faryes* do the Meadows till,
>   More by their presence then their skill.
> Their Statues polish'd by some ancient hand,
>   May to adorn the Gardens stand:

> But howso'ere the Figures do excel,
> The *Gods* themselves with us do dwell.

Marvell has in his poetry many other symbols of this kind of "fragrant Innocence," always threatened or overcome by some corruption. Thus even the small girl whom he celebrates in "The Picture of little T. C. in a Prospect of Flowers" must grow up, damage mankind by her beauty, and then die, despite her Eden-like beginning:

> See with what simplicity
> This Nimph begins her golden daies!
> In the green Grass she loves to lie,
> And there with her fair Aspect tames
> The Wilder flow'rs, and gives them names:
> But only with the Roses playes;
> And them does tell
> What Colour best becomes them, and what Smell.

Like Adam she names the other creatures, and as with Adam the world of mortality awaits her, as Marvell makes plain in the last stanza:

> But O young beauty of the Woods,
> Whom Nature courts with fruits and flow'rs,
> Gather the Flow'rs, but spare the Buds;
> Lest *Flora* angry at thy crime,
> To kill her Infants in their prime,
> Do quickly make th'Example Yours;
> And, ere we see,
> Nip in the blossome all our hopes and Thee.

Thus in one way or another she is threatened with the fate that has overtaken the innocent Nymph who complains for the death of her fawn in the enigmatic, fascinating poem that has attracted so much attention by critics and scholars of this century, beginning with Eliot's remark in his fine essay on Marvell:

> Marvell takes a slight affair, the feeling of a girl for her pet, and gives it a connexion with that inexhaustible and terrible nebula of emotion which surrounds all our exact and practical passions and mingles with them.[12]

Everyone agrees that the poem must have some symbolic significance—but hardly anyone agrees on what this is.[13] It seems to have some local significance for the English Civil Wars in its opening lines:

> The wanton Troopers riding by
> Have shot my Faun and it will dye.

The Troopers are the marauding cavalrymen of the Civil Wars, on both sides, for the word "Troopers" was a general term: one could speak of Cromwell's Troopers or of Prince Rupert's Troopers.[14] In either case they are wanton in their unruly lack of discipline, in their carelessness of others' rights. But what does the fawn represent? Some have found in him the symbolism of Christ, since the Nymph says

> There is not such another in
> The World, to offer for their Sin.

And a little later she echoes the phrase of Jeremiah (2:2) when she says that the fawn "seem'd to bless/Its self in me." These religious implications are enforced by the garden imagery that follows a little later, imagery that clearly echoes the Song of Solomon, particularly the verses:

> My beloved is gone down into his garden,
> to the beds of spices, to feed in the gardens,
> and to gather lilies.
>
> I am my beloved's, and my beloved is mine:
> he feedeth among the lilies.   (6:2–3)

So we find the fawn in a garden of roses and lilies, and the Nymph says:

> Among the beds of Lillyes, I
> Have sought it oft, where it should lye;

and she finds the fawn feeding upon the roses. The purity of the fawn, and the fact that it dies "as calmly as a Saint," have led some to see in the poem profound Christian implications. But on the other hand the pagan and classical implications are equally strong: similar stories about the deaths of pet deer occur in Vergil and Ovid;[15] the Nymph's tears will be placed "in *Diana's* Shrine," and the fawn will go to a pagan Elizium. The Nymph imagines herself turned into a statue like that of Niobe, forever weeping. Furthermore, she is not weeping just for her pet deer, but also for the faithless man who gave him to her: "unconstant *Sylvio*," a seducer who talks the old Petrarchan sweet talk:

> Said He, look how your Huntsman here
> Hath taught a Faun to hunt his *Dear*.

The point is that the fawn and the Nymph are both destroyed by "false and cruel men," and the whole poem thus
becomes a lament for lost innocence, whether destroyed by
war or by human infidelity, whether it exists in pagan or in
Christian story. Wanton men kill the very innocence that
prays for their salvation.

The end of innocence, the destruction of the pastoral garden, and the search for their recovery in the mind—these are
Marvell's deepest themes. His abrasive political satires and his
great political poems on Cromwell have all been made possible
by the existence of the interior retreat which he describes in
the latter half of his long pastoral poem, "Upon Appleton
House." Here in the fourth section of that poem (which is
clearly divisible into six main parts: the House, the History,
the Garden, the Meadow, the Wood, and the Vision of Maria)
the speaker's mind plays over the meadow, inventing from its
images a fanciful entertainment, a theatrical presentation of
worldly scenes, a playful nightmare, where at first man seems
to drown in the abyss of greenness:

> To see Men through this Meadow Dive,
> We wonder how they rise alive.

It is a world of flux and change, mingling images of the ideal
and the actual, creating a "scene" that seems to change by
some mechanical devices such as were used by Inigo Jones in
the Court entertainments that we have discussed:

> No Scene that turns with Engines strange
> Does oftner then these Meadows change.
> For when the Sun the Grass hath vext,
> The tawny Mowers enter next;

Enter, that is, like theatrical performers. And as they mow the meadows we have suggestions of blood and death as the edge of the scythe cuts into the peaceful birds nesting on the ground. Then another change brings in a battle scene, intricately "wrought":

> The Mower now commands the Field;
> In whose new Traverse seemeth wrought
> A Camp of Battail newly fought:
> Where, as the Meads with Hay, the Plain
> Lyes quilted ore with Bodies slain:
> The Women that with forks it fling,
> Do represent the Pillaging.

The word "traverse" means literally the action of the mowers as they make their ways back and forth across the field; but "traverse" in the language of Marvell's time could also mean a curtain. It is upon this curtain, as though it were a tapestry, that the "Camp of Battail" is "wrought," "Camp" being used here in the old sense of *champ*, that is, a field of battle, as the word "Plain" in the next line makes clear. In this curiously inverted analogy, Marvell is saying that as on some great curtain, the Meads are quilted over with fallen hay just as on a battlefield the plain "Lyes quilted ore with Bodies slain"—the word "quilted," of course, carrying on the imagery of handicraft and artifact. At the same time it is relevant to feel something of the military sense of the word "traverse," which means, of course, a barrier in a fortification. Finally, the word "represent" in the last line carries on the imagery of theater or tapestry.

In spite of these threats, however, it is all only a harmless pastoral scene, as the next stanza tells us:

> And now the careless Victors play,
> Dancing the Triumphs of the Hay;

(With a pun on the word *hay*, meaning also a rustic dance)

> Where every Mowers wholesome Heat
> Smells like an *Alexanders sweat*.
> Their Females fragrant as the Mead
> Which they in *Fairy Circles* tread:
> When at their Dances End they kiss,
> Their new-made Hay not sweeter is.

Pastoral, yes, but as we continue reading we find that further hints of the world of time and death are brought in, as the hay suggests to the poet a resemblance to Pyramids on the "*Desert Memphis Sand*," and also to the Roman camps which rise "In Hills for Soldiers Obsequies." But again the scene changes as the next stanza shows:

> This *Scene* again withdrawing brings
> A new and empty Face of things;
> A levell'd space, as smooth and plain,
> As Clothes for *Lilly* strecht to stain.

The reference to the paintings of Sir Peter Lely maintains the vision seen through the world of art forms, but soon the

actual world comes in upon this levelled space as the poet
mentions the bull-ring at Madrid, or sees in the field a pattern
for "the *Levellers*," that radical left-wing sect which threatened the hierarchies of society in Marvell's day.

Thus throughout the contemplation of the meadow a conflict is set up between the imagery of art forms and the actuality of war and death, as though the pastoral scene were living
on the verge of destruction—and then suddenly it is destroyed,
as a flood overtakes this "painted World":

> Then, to conclude these pleasant Acts,
> *Denton* sets ope its *Cataracts*;
> And makes the Meadow truly be
> (What it but seem'd before) a Sea.

In the midst of this comical catastrophe, while the whole
world turns topsy-turvy, we discover that behind the Mannerist facade of art lies something deeper:

> But I, retiring from the Flood,
> Take Sanctuary in the Wood;
> And, while it lasts, my self imbark
> In this yet green, yet growing Ark;

It is the ark of the contemplative mind, where the poet (wittily, with a play on the word "imbark") finds his refuge;
although even here nature is fallen, as the woodpecker knows,
acting as moral judge of the world within the wood:

> He walks still upright from the Root,
> Meas'ring the Timber with his Foot;
> And all the way, to keep it clean,
> Doth from the Bark the Wood-moths glean.

He, with his Beak, examines well
Which fit to stand and which to fell.

The good he numbers up, and hacks;
As if he mark'd them with the Ax.
But where he, tinkling with his Beak,
Does find the hollow Oak to speak,
That for his building he designs,
And through the tainted Side he mines.
Who could have thought the *tallest Oak*
Should fall by such a *feeble Strok*'!

Nor would it, had the Tree not fed
A *Traitor-worm*, within it bred.
(As first our *Flesh* corrupt within
Tempts impotent and bashful *Sin*.)

The whole passage, particularly the witty inversion of the
relationship between flesh and sin in the last two lines, gives
a clear instance of Marvell's unique tone of serious wit, of
playful morality, the tone that Eliot long ago gave its classic
description, when he spoke of Marvell's wit as maintaining
"this alliance of levity and seriousness (by which the seriousness is intensified)."[16] Then Marvell sums up this attitude in
two lines:

Thus I, *easie Philosopher*,
Among the *Birds* and *Trees* confer:

Easie is the right word, meaning, at ease, detached from care,
free from pain, annoyance, or burden, free from pressure
or hurry. The poet's mind is wholly in harmony with nature,
and as he reads thus "in *Natures mystick Book*" the artifice

of the theater is turned into the robes of nature herself as the speaker is garbed with a costume that reminds one of some Court Masquer:

> And see how Chance's better Wit
> Could with a Mask my studies hit!
> The Oak-Leaves me embroyder all,
> Between which Caterpillars crawl:
> And Ivy, with familiar trails,
> Me licks, and clasps, and curles, and hales.
> Under this *antick Cope* I move
> Like some great *Prelate of the Grove*,

(*Antick:* meaning both "fantastic," as in a masque, and "antique.")

This then is the center of the mind's security, as the poet lives in physical and mental harmony:

> How safe, methinks, and strong, behind
> These Trees have I incamp'd my Mind;
> Where Beauty, aiming at the Heart,
> Bends in some Tree its useless Dart;
> And where the World no certain Shot
> Can make, or me it toucheth not.
> But I on it securely play,
> And gaul its Horsemen all the Day.

(A foreshadowing of the time when Marvell's satires will play their bitter wit against the leaders of Charles II's regime.) And finally, this natural harmony reaches its climax in a pastoral ecstasy, as the speaker implies his realization that he cannot stay forever in this sanctuary, through his hyperbolic imagery of joyous bondage and happy crucifixion:

Bind me ye *Woodbines* in your 'twines,
Curle me about ye gadding *Vines*,
And Oh so close your Circles lace,
That I may never leave this Place:
But, lest your Fetters prove too weak,
Ere I your Silken Bondage break,
Do you, O *Brambles*, chain me too,
And courteous *Briars* nail me through.

Now, gradually, we become aware that in the poet's vision
the outer world itself has undergone a magical transformation:

For now the Waves are fal'n and dry'd,
And now the Meadows fresher dy'd;
Whose Grass, with moister colour dasht,
Seems as green Silks but newly washt.

In this renewed world there comes to complete the scene the
perfection of human beauty and virtue in the figure of the
young Fairfax daughter, Marvell's student, who by a fortunate coincidence is named Mary. Calling her by the name
Maria, Marvell universalizes the young girl into a figure of the
highest humanity, and declares, through hyperbolic rhetoric,
that this virtuous human beauty is necessary to unify and
perfect the created world:

'Tis *She* that to these Gardens gave
That wondrous Beauty which they have;
She streightness on the Woods bestows;
To *Her* the Meadow sweetness owes;
Nothing could make the River be

> So Chrystal-pure but only *She*;
> *She* yet more Pure, Sweet, Streight, and Fair,
> Then Gardens, Woods, Meads, Rivers are.

But as he recapitulates the scenes of his poem he insists that human nature must rise above even these superb physical beauties, for the perfection of human nature lies in heavenly wisdom:

> For *She*, to higher Beauties rais'd,
> Disdains to be for lesser prais'd.
> *She* counts her Beauty to converse
> In all the Languages as *hers*;
> Nor yet in those *her self* imployes
> But for the *Wisdome*, not the *Noyse*;
> Nor yet that *Wisdome* would affect,
> But as 'tis *Heavens Dialect*.

Grasping thus in imagination the vision of an ideal harmony of the natural and the human, Marvell is able to see the whole estate as an image of interior restoration:

> 'Tis not, what once it was, the *World*;
> But a rude heap together hurl'd;
> All negligently overthrown,
> Gulfes, Deserts, Precipices, Stone.
> Your lesser *World* contains the same.
> But in more decent Order tame;
> *You Heaven's Center, Nature's Lap.*
> *And Paradice's only Map.*

The words apply to the estate, to Mary, and to the inner condition of the speaker himself. At the close of this long, pastoral-meditative work, Marvell has attained an ideal vision by creating, for a time, a vision of nature seen through the lens of art, with an effect of "dream-like sublimation or high-spirited play," in the words of Arnold Hauser.[17] Thus Marvell's "Upon Appleton House" may be said to represent, better than any other English poem, the "revolution in sensibility" which Hauser has found in Mannerism:

> The essential to be borne in mind is the heterogeneous and contradictory nature of reality as seen by mannerism in general. In mannerist art things are seen alternately in concrete and abstract form, now as substantial, now as insubstantial, and now one and now the other aspect is uppermost. Appearance and reality, truth and illusion are inextricably interwoven, and we live in a borderland of wakefulness and dream, knowledge and intuition, sensuous and ideal awareness; it is this that matters, not precise determination of the boundaries between the various provinces of being. The point is the difference between the two worlds we belong to, between which there is no making any final and exclusive choice . . .[18]

Notes

Notes

NOTES FOR JOHN DONNE

1. Edmund Gosse, *The Life and Letters of John Donne*, 2 vols. (London, Heinemann, 1899), II, 360–63.

2. See John Bryson, "Lost Portrait of Donne," *Times* (London), 13 Oct. 1959, pp. 13, 15. Also Helen Gardner, "The Marshall Engraving and the Lothian Portrait," in her edition of Donne's *Elegies and Songs and Sonnets* (Oxford, Clarendon Press, 1965), Appendix E. I am indebted to both of these essays for some of the details concerning Donne's portraits. See also the "Iconography" in Geoffrey Keynes, *A Bibliography of Dr. John Donne*, 3rd edn. (Cambridge University Press, 1958), pp. 265–68.

3. For evidence that the wide-brimmed hat and folded arms are signs of the melancholy lover see Bryson and Gardner (above, n.2); also Roy Strong, "The Elizabethan Malady: Melancholy in Elizabethan and Jacobean Portraiture," *Apollo*, 79 (April, 1964), pp. 264–69. One should add the striking analogy with Donne's posture and costume found in Inigo Jones's drawing of a melancholy lover for Ben Jonson's masque *Loves Triumph through Callipolis* (1631); see the description by Percy Simpson and C. F. Bell, *Designs by Inigo Jones for Masques & Plays at Court* (Oxford, 1924), Walpole Society, vol. 12, p. 55,

no. 77; this is reproduced in Enid Welsford, *The Court Masque* (Cambridge University Press, 1927), facing p. 216.

4. Bryson (above, n. 2) quotes the Latin passage from the *Breviary*, but locates it in the third Collect for Evening Prayer; this is correct for the English service, but the Latin source is in the service for Compline: see F. E. Brightman, *The English Rite*, 2nd edn., 2 vols. (London, 1921), I, 164; and *Portiforium seu Breviarium ad usum ecclesie Sarisburiensis . . . Pars Hyemalis* (Paris, Regnault, 1554), "Preces completorii," f. 69v. See also Ps. 17:29: "Quoniam tu illuminas lucernam meam, Domine: Deus meus, illumina tenebras meas;" and 2 Kings 22:29: "et tu, Domine, illuminabis tenebras meas."

5. Izaak Walton, *Lives*, World's Classics edn. (Oxford University Press, 1927), p. 78.

6. Bryson's remark concerning the Lothian portrait (above, n. 2) is most astute: "Nor is it without interest that he should to the end of his life have preserved this image of his youthful self. The picture with its inscription must have been hanging in a neighbouring room in the Deanery when that 'choice painter' was summoned to the death-bed to make the last terrible portrait of the poet in his shroud."

7. Quotations from Donne's poetry are given according to the text of the new Clarendon Press edition of Donne: *Divine Poems*, ed. Helen Gardner, 1952; *Elegies and Songs and Sonnets*, ed. Helen Gardner, 1965; *Satires, Epigrams, and Verse Letters*, ed. W. Milgate, 1967. I am throughout this lecture indebted to the admirable introductions and commentaries in these volumes.

8. Walton, *Lives*, p. 37.

9. See Abraham Van der Doort, *Catalogue of the Collections of Charles I*, ed. Oliver Millar (Glasgow, 1960), Walpole Society, vol. 37, p. 89, item 71: "And the other of your Majesty's pictures was done by Titian, being our Lady and Christ and St. John half figures as big as the life, which was placed in your Majesty's middle privy lodging room being in a carved gilded frame, and was given heretofore to your Majesty by my lord of Carlisle who had it of Doctor Donne; painted upon the right

light." (I have here modernized the text.) This may be the item mentioned in the second paragraph of my previous quotation from Donne's will: see W. Milgate, "Dr. Donne's Art Gallery," *Notes and Queries*, 194 (1949), pp. 318–19. Like Milgate, I have not been able to identify this painting.

10. See *The Age of the Renaissance*, ed. Denys Hay (New York, McGraw-Hill, 1967), p. 132; a superb color-reproduction of the painting is given here, along with the explanation, forming part of Roberto Weiss's chapter, "The New Learning." I have followed Weiss in most of the details.

11. Some good manuscripts of Donne read "Ragged" instead of "Cragged" in line 80 of Satire III. Milgate regards "Ragged" as an authentic reading of an earlier version of this line: see his edition of the *Satires*, p. 146.

12. See the interesting analysis of this poem by Helen Gardner, *The Business of Criticism* (Oxford, Clarendon Press, 1959), pp. 62–75.

13. *Poems of John Donne*, ed. Herbert J. C. Grierson, 2 vols. (Oxford, Clarendon Press, 1912), II, 31. *Elegies and Songs and Sonnets*, ed. Gardner, p. 207.

14. Izaak Walton says the poem was given by Donne to his wife when he went abroad with Sir Robert Drury, i.e., in 1611 (*Lives*, p. 42). The point is not essential, though the situation seems plausible to me. But see Miss Gardner's contrary arguments in her edition of the *Elegies and Songs and Sonnets*, p. xxix.

15. See George Williamson, "The Convention of *The Extasie*," in his *Seventeenth Century Contexts* (University of Chicago Press, 1961), pp. 63–77.

16. See the illuminating account of the poem's relation to the *Dialoghi* of Leone Ebreo by Helen Gardner, "The Argument about 'The Ecstasy,'" in *Elizabethan and Jacobean Studies Presented to Frank Percy Wilson* (Oxford, Clarendon Press, 1959), pp. 279–306; also the study of the poem in relation to a number of Renaissance philosophers of love in Italy, by A. J. Smith, "The Metaphysic of Love," *Review of English Studies*, n.s. 9 (1958), pp. 362–75.

17. See Miss Gardner's account of the five manuscripts that constitute "Group I" in her edition of Donne's *Divine Poems*, pp. lvii–lxvi. One of the most interesting aspects of Miss Gardner's analysis is her evidence that this group of manuscripts may derive from the collection of Donne's poems that we know Donne himself was making in 1614, just before he entered the priesthood. A study of these five manuscripts leaves me with the conviction that Miss Gardner's hypothesis is the only possible conclusion. The arrangement of the love-songs in "Group I" forms the core of the traditional order (or disorder) of the "Songs and Sonets," as they have come down to us through the editions of 1633, 1635, and Grierson (though the editor of 1635 removed "The Flea" from its manuscript position and placed it first in the section that he presented under the title "Songs and Sonets").

The contents and order of the section devoted to the love-songs in "Group I" have been very closely followed by John Shawcross in his recent edition of Donne's *Complete Poetry*, New York, Doubleday, Anchor Books, 1967. In Shawcross's numbering, poems 25 through 71 (beginning with "The Message" and ending with "The Dampe") follow almost exactly the order of the Dowden and St. Paul's mss. (for slight variations in the other three "Group I" mss. see Miss Gardner's account in *Divine Poems*, p. lix). But there are two exceptions: poem 26 in Shawcross, "Witchcraft by a Picture," is not a part of "Group I" (though it is added by a different hand on a blank page of the Leconfield ms.); and after poem 51, "Twicknam Garden," the two-part "Epitaph" is found in three of the "Group I" mss.

As Miss Gardner notes in her edition of the *Elegies and Songs and Sonnets* (p. lxv, n. 2), nine of Donne's love-songs are missing in "Group I": six of the lesser poems ("love-epigrams", as Miss Gardner calls them), and three of Donne's more important poems: "Farewell to Love," "A Nocturnal upon St. Lucy's Day," and "The Dissolution." The first of these, Donne's most bitter poem of sexual disillusionment, may well have been omitted for reasons of propriety; the other two, poems lamenting the death of the beloved lady, may both have been written after the death of Donne's wife in 1617.

18. See *Elegies and Songs and Sonnets*, ed. Gardner, pp. xxxi–ii.

19. *Ibid.*, p. 150.

20. This two-part poem is omitted from the Cambridge University Library ms. (Add. Ms. 5778), and the Leconfield ms., belonging to Sir Geoffrey Keynes.

Among the vast number of books and articles on Donne, I wish to express a general appreciation of insights gained from the following: Pierre Legouis, *Donne the Craftsman*, Paris, Didier, 1928; C. S. Lewis, "Donne and Love Poetry in the Seventeenth Century," and Joan Bennett, "The Love Poetry of John Donne, A Reply to Mr. C. S. Lewis," in *Seventeenth-Century Studies Presented to Sir Herbert Grierson* (Oxford, Clarendon Press, 1938), pp. 64–104; Leonard Unger, *Donne's Poetry and Modern Criticism*, Chicago, Regnery, 1950; J. B. Leishman, *The Monarch of Wit*, London, Hutchinson, 1951; Clay Hunt, *Donne's Poetry*, New Haven, Yale University Press, 1954; *The Songs and Sonets of John Donne*, ed. Theodore Redpath, London, Methuen, 1956; Arnold Stein, *John Donne's Lyrics*, Minneapolis, University of Minnesota Press, 1962.

NOTES FOR THOMAS CAREW

1. Quotations from Carew's poetry are taken from *The Poems of Thomas Carew, with his Masque Coelum Britannicum*, ed. Rhodes Dunlap, Oxford, Clarendon Press, 1949; I am throughout this lecture indebted to Dunlap's introduction and commentary.

2. The text of *Salmacida Spolia* (ed. T. J. B. Spencer) is available in *A Book of Masques, in Honour of Allardyce Nicoll* (Cambridge University Press, 1967), pp. 337–70; for my quotations see pp. 347, 357–8. Many of Inigo Jones's drawings for *Salmacida Spolia* are handsomely reproduced in *Festival Designs by Inigo Jones: Drawings for Scenery & Costume from the Devonshire Collection, Chatsworth*, Introduction and Catalogue by Roy Strong, Foreword by Thomas S. Wragg (International Exhibitions Foundation, 1967), plates 90–103. See the full catalogue of the Jones drawings at Chatsworth: Percy Simpson and C. F. Bell, *Designs by Inigo Jones for Masques & Plays at Court* (Oxford, 1924), Walpole Society, vol. 12; with many illustrations. Also Allardyce Nicoll, *Stuart Masques and the Renaissance Stage*, New York, Harcourt, Brace and Co., 1938; with many illustrations.

3. *The Dramatic Records of Sir Henry Herbert*, ed. Joseph Quincy Adams (New Haven, Yale University Press, 1917), p. 55. For extracts from contemporary documents concerning the production of Carew's masque see Gerald Eades Bentley, *The Jacobean and Caroline Stage*, 7 vols. (Oxford, Clarendon Press, 1941–68), III, 106–10. For Inigo Jones's drawings for this masque see Simpson and Bell, *Designs*, Nos. 191–209.

4. *Poems of Carew*, ed. Dunlap, p. 177.

5. *Ibid.*, pp. 178–9.

6. Townshend's poem to Carew is printed in *Poems of Carew*, ed. Dunlap, pp. 207–8. My dating of Carew's poem depends upon the reference to Montagu's *Shepheards Paradise*, produced on January 9, 1633. Of course, the elaborate preparations for this play were discussed at Court throughout the preceding Fall: see Bentley, *op. cit.*, IV, 917–21; the Queen and her Ladies were reported as already "practising" their parts by September 20, 1632. Carew may well have seen rehearsals; but his poem seems to be describing a full-scale performance of some kind. Townshend's verse-letter speaks of how "the windes from every corner bring/ The too true nuse of the dead conquering king." Allowing several weeks for this "news" to reach England, one might

wish to date Carew's answer in late November or in December, 1632. On the other hand, if Townshend was writing around to his friends to collect a group of elegies, he might well have been doing this in January. A collection of ten elegies on Gustavus Adolphus was in fact published in *The Swedish Intelligencer*, Third Part, London, 1633; all of these are printed anonymously, except for one by Henry King.

7. See Bentley, *op. cit.*, IV, 918; Simpson and Bell, *Designs*, Nos. 163–79.

8. *Poems of Carew*, ed. Dunlap, p. 252.

9. See *Aurelian Townshend's Poems and Masks*, ed. E. K. Chambers (Oxford, Clarendon Press, 1912), pp. 90–91:

> In the midst of the ayre the eight *Spheares* in rich habites were seated on a Cloud, which in a circular forme was on each side continued unto the highest part of the Heaven, and seem'd to have let them downe as in a Chaine.
>
> To the Musicke of these Spheares there appear'd two other Clouds descending, & in them were discovered eight Stars; these being come to the middle Region of the skie, another greater Cloud came downe above them; Which by little and little descending, discovered other glistering Stars to the number of sixe: and above all in a Chariot of gold-smithes workes richly adorned with precious Iemmes, sat divine Beauty, over whose head, appear'd a brightnesse, full of small starres that inviron'd the top of the Chariot, striking a light round about it. . . ,
>
> This sight altogether was for the difficulty of the Ingining and number of the persons the greatest that hath beene seene here in our time. For the apparitions of such as came downe in the ayre, and the *Choruses* standing beneath arrived to the number of fifty persons all richly attired, shewing the magnificence of the Court of *England*.

See Simpson and Bell, *Designs*, Nos. 139–62.

10. Townshend, *Poems and Masks*, ed. Chambers, p. 93.

11. *Ibid.*, p. 96: "the *Eagle* with *Iove* flew up, and *Cupid* tooke his flight through the Ayre, after which the Heavens close."

12. The whole fourth Act of *The Shepheards Paradise* is full of abstract conversation about the pure and spiritual nature of Love, and at the beginning of the fifth Act, Genorio exclaims:

Me-thinks I find my mind on wing, loose from my senses, which like limed twigs held it till now. It is so light, and so ascensive now, it meanes to work it selfe above *Martiroes*. I am already so farre towards it, as the beliefe that I did never love till now. O how I was deceived, while I conceived that Love was so Materiall it could be touched, and grasp't! I find it an undepending ayrinesse that both supports, and fills it selfe, and is to be felt by what it nourisheth, no more then aire, whose virtue onely we discerne.

Shepheards Paradise (1659), p. 110.

13. *Ibid.*, p. 112. Bentley (*op. cit.*, IV, 918) quotes a contemporary as reporting that the Queen, in her performance of *The Shepheards Paradise*, "is said to have herself excelled really all others both in acting *and singing*" (my italics).

14. Townshend, *Poems and Masks,* ed. Chambers, p. 13; taken from Henry Lawes, *The Second Book of Ayres and Dialogues,* 1655, where the song is attributed to Townshend.

15. Folger ms. 4462: see Bentley, *op. cit.*, IV, 920; and G. Thorn-Drury, *A Little Ark, Containing Sundry Pieces of Seventeenth-Century Verse* (London, Dobell, 1921), pp. 4–7, where Thorn-Drury prints the Prologue and four songs that occur between the acts; the Folger ms. was then in Thorn-Drury's possession.

16. Thus Townshend's work might be said to "comprise" (comprehend, contain, sum up) "the beauties of the *SHEP-HERDS PARADISE*." In this connection, Erica Veevers has called attention to the existence in the Huntington Library of a printed fragment or synopsis of a pastoral masque by Townshend that seems to bear a close relation to *The Shepheards Paradise*. She suggests that Townshend may have written this entertainment "to complement a performance of Montagu's play." See *Notes and Queries,* 210 (1965), pp. 343–5. (The fragment by Townshend is also described by Bentley, *op. cit.*, V, 1231.) See also the rejoinder by Paulina Palmer (*Notes and Queries,* 211 [1966], pp. 303–4), who calls attention to Townshend's poem in praise of the Queen's singing. Since there appear to have been at least two performances of *The Shepheards Paradise*, there

is room to conjecture several occasions on which Montagu's play may have been enhanced by Townshend's aid.

17. See the interpretation of this painting by Erwin Panofsky, *Studies in Iconology*, Harper Torchbooks (New York, Harper and Row, 1962), pp. 86–91 (originally pub. by Oxford University Press, 1939).

18. John Shearman, *Mannerism* (London, Penguin Books, 1967), pp. 15–30.

19. See the analysis of this poem by Edward I. Selig, *The Flourishing Wreath. A Study of Thomas Carew's Poetry* (New Haven, Yale University Press, 1958), pp. 150–60; this whole book has many fine insights into Carew's poetry. See also the excellent series of articles by Rufus Blanshard: "Carew and Jonson," *Studies in Philology*, 52 (1955), pp. 195–211; "Thomas Carew and the Cavalier Poets," *Transactions of the Wisconsin Academy*, 43 (1954), pp. 97–105; "Thomas Carew's Master Figures," *Boston University Studies in English*, 3 (1957), pp. 214–27. See also the chapter by George Williamson, "The Fringe of the Tradition," in *The Donne Tradition*, Cambridge, Harvard University Press, 1930; and the classic essay by F. R. Leavis, "The Line of Wit," in *Revaluation* (London, Chatto and Windus, 1936), esp. p. 38, with its witty summation of the eclectic effects of Carew's epitaph on Maria Wentworth: "It opens in the manner of Ben Jonson's Epitaphs. The conceit in the second stanza is both Jonson and Donne, and the third stanza is specifically Metaphysical. After the Augustan passage we come to the Caroline wit of the 'chaste Poligamie.' And we end with a line in Marvell's characteristic movement . . . ."

20. Dunlap (*Poems of Carew*, p. 251) notes the echo of the opening lines of *I Henry IV:* ". . . Finde we a time for frighted Peace to pant,/ And breath shortwinded accents of new broils . . ." One should note too the echo of Donne's *First Anniversary* (67–73), esp. of Donne's phrase "A faint weake love of vertue" (71). See also Donne's *Second Anniversary* (6–7): "But as a ship which hath strooke saile, doth runne/ By force of that force which before, it wonne."

21. See Ruth C. Wallerstein, "The Development of the Rhetoric and Metre of the Heroic Couplet, Especially in 1625–1645," *PMLA*, 50 (1935), pp. 166–209; esp. pp. 186–93 for the influence of Sandys's Ovid and paraphrase of Job.

22. See Dunlap's "Note on the Musical Settings of Carew's Poems," in his edition of Carew, pp. 289–93.

23. See Dunlap's many analogies in the notes to his edition of Carew.

NOTES FOR RICHARD CRASHAW

1. Roy Daniells, *Milton, Mannerism and Baroque*, University of Toronto Press, 1963.

2. See Rudolf Wittkower, *Gian Lorenzo Bernini*, 2nd edn. (London, Phaidon Press, 1966), p. 19.

3. *The Flaming Hart or the Life of the Glorious S. Teresa* (Antwerp, 1642), pp. 419–20; the translation is attributed to Sir Toby Matthew.

4. See the superb accounts by Rudolf Wittkower, *Art and Architecture in Italy: 1600 to 1750*, 2nd edn. (Penguin Books, 1965), pp. 103–5; and *Bernini*, pp. 25–6, with the painting of the entire chapel, facing p. 28.

5. Quotations from Crashaw are taken from the text in *The Anchor Anthology of Seventeenth Century Verse*, Vol. I, ed. Martz, New York, Doubleday, Anchor Books, 1969; this text is based on the second edition of Crashaw's *Steps to the Temple*, London, 1648, with certain readings and additional lines drawn from the posthumous edition of Crashaw's poems, *Carmen Deo Nostro*, edited by Thomas Car and published in Paris, 1652.

6. See Jacobus de Wit, *De Kerken Van Antwerpen*, ed. J. de Bosschere (Antwerp, 1910), p. 104; and J. B. Descamps, *Voyage Pittoresque de la Flandre et du Brabant* (Paris, 1769), p. 181. I am grateful to Dr. A. Monballieu, of the Antwerp Museum, for pointing out these references to me.

7. I know this version only from a monochrome photograph provided by the courtesy of Fondation Cultura, Brussels, and l'Institut Royal du Patrimoine Artistique, Brussels. A letter from the English Convent to Fondation Cultura gives the information that, in comparison with a photograph of the Antwerp painting, the Bruges version is darker in its colors and slightly larger, both in length and in breadth. One can see from the monochrome photograph that a much larger expanse of wing is shown for the angel at the left in the Bruges version, while the whole painting is slightly extended on the other three edges. The difference in size may be due to framing, now, or in the past. I have made an effort to see this version in Bruges, but was unable to do so, since the picture is placed in the nun's enclosure. A large reproduction of the Antwerp version in full color is available in the portfolio published by Cultura: *Rubens en de Barokschilderkunst* (*Kŭnst in België* VI), Plate 42.

8. See Joseph Anthony Mazzeo, "A Seventeenth-Century Theory of Metaphysical Poetry," and "Metaphysical Poetry and the Poetic of Correspondence," in his *Renaissance and Seventeenth-Century Studies* (New York, Columbia University Press, 1964), pp. 29–59.

9. For a careful account of Seghers, with numerous illustrations, see D. Roggen and H. Pauwels, "Het Caravaggistisch Oeuvre van Gerard Zegers," *Gentse Bijdragen Tot de Kunstgeschiedenis*, 16 (1955–56), pp. 255–301. The authors would date the St. Teresa painting in the years 1625–30, during Seghers' period of transition from *caravagisme* to *l'esprit rubénien*.

10. A. F. Allison, "Some Influences in Crashaw's Poem 'On a Prayer Booke Sent to Mrs. M. R.,'" *Review of English Studies*, 23 (1947), 34–42; see pp. 41–2 for parallels with Carew's "A Rapture."

11. Robert Southwell, *Marie Magdalens Funeral Teares* (London, 1591), Preface.

12. See the important essay by Mario Praz, "The Flaming Heart: Richard Crashaw and the Baroque," *The Flaming Heart* (New York: Doubleday, Anchor Books, 1958), pp. 204–63; see

pp. 218–26 for comments on "The Weeper."

13. See my study *The Poetry of Meditation*, 2nd edn. (New Haven, Yale University Press, 1962), pp. 331–52.

I wish to acknowledge a general debt to the classic study by Austin Warren, *Richard Crashaw: A Study in Baroque Sensibility*, Louisiana State University Press, 1939; and to the introduction and commentary in L. C. Martin's edition of Crashaw's *Poems*, 2nd edn., Oxford, Clarendon Press, 1957.

NOTES FOR ANDREW MARVELL

1. Quotations from Marvell's poetry are taken from *The Poems & Letters of Andrew Marvell*, ed. H. M. Margoliouth, 2nd edn., 2 vols., Oxford, Clarendon Press, 1952. I am indebted to the commentary in this edition.

2. See the interesting discussion of this and other pastoral poems of Marvell by Edward William Tayler in his chapter "Marvell's Garden of the Mind," *Nature and Art in Renaissance Literature*, New York, Columbia University Press, 1964.

3. For detailed discussion of this controversial point see my note in *The Anchor Anthology of Seventeenth-Century Verse*, I, 487; and the philological support for this argument given by George Lord in his admirable new edition, *Andrew Marvell: Complete Poetry* (New York, Modern Library, 1968), p. 24.

4. Arnold Hauser, *Mannerism: The Crisis of the Renaissance and the Origin of Modern Art*, 2 vols., London, Routledge and Kegan Paul, 1965.

5. *Ibid.*, I, 12–13.

6. *Ibid.*, I, 13.

7. See Crashaw's "Ode which was prefixed to a Prayer booke given to a young Gentlewoman," 77–8. Also the great passage at the close of Sir Thomas Browne's *Urne Buriall:* "And if any have been so happy as truly to understand Christian annihilation,

extasis, exolution, liquefaction, transformation, the kisse of the Spouse, gustation of God, and ingression into the divine shadow, they have already had an handsome anticipation of heaven; the glory of the world is surely over, and the earth in ashes unto them." (*Urne Buriall,* ed. John Carter, Cambridge University Press, 1958, p. 50.)

8. Jean H. Hagstrum, *The Sister Arts* (University of Chicago Press, 1958), pp. 114–17. See also the comment on "The Gallery" by Frank J. Warnke, "Play and Metamorphosis in Marvell's Poetry," *Studies in English Literature,* 5 (1965), pp. 23–30.

9. I have explored some aspects of this quest in *The Paradise Within: Studies in Vaughan, Traherne, and Milton,* New Haven, Yale University Press, 1964.

10. See the recent study by John R. Cooper, *The Art of The Compleat Angler,* Durham, N. C., Duke University Press, 1968.

11. Cf. Tayler, *op. cit.,* p. 159.

12. T. S. Eliot, *Selected Essays, 1917–1932* (New York, Harcourt, Brace and Co., 1932), p. 259.

13. The controversy has been admirably summed up, with full references, by Earl Miner, "The Death of Innocence in Marvell's *Nymph Complaining for the Death of her Faun,*" *Modern Philology,* 65 (1967), pp. 9–16, and by Ruth Nevo, "Marvell's 'Songs of Innocence and Experience,' " *Studies in English Literature,* 5(1965), pp. 1–21. I agree with the view that the theme of the poem is "the death of innocence," but cannot accept Miner's suggestion that the poem may also carry political implications related to the destruction of the old order by Parliamentary forces. A number of readers have, I think, been misled by the account of the word "troopers" in the *OED,* where we are told: "The term was used in connexion with the Covenanting Army which invaded England in 1640." But, as my next note makes clear, the word was also being used in the 1640's to apply to Royalist "Troopers."

14. See the use of the word "Troopers" in *The Parliaments Vindication, in Answer to Prince Ruperts Declaration, by S. W.,* London, 1642. This pamphlet reprints and answers the *Declaration*

in which Prince Rupert defends his army against the charge of committing atrocities: "But since it hath pleased my Lord Wharton to tell the whole City of London openly at Guild-hall, and since to tell it all the world in print, that one great cause of their preservation at Edge-hill, was the barbarousnesse and inhumanity of Prince Rupert and his Troopers, that we spared neither man, woman, nor childe . . . ." S. W. in his reply refers to "the barbarous inhumanity of Prince *Ruperts* troopers." (I owe this reference to my friend Daniel Woodward.)

15. Several commentators have pointed out analogies with the story of the stag of Cyparissus in the *Metamorphoses*, X, 106–42, and with the story of Silvia's deer killed by Ascanius, *Aeneid*, VII, 475–510. (See Miner, *op. cit.*, p. 13.)

16. T. S. Eliot, *op. cit.*, p. 255.

17. Hauser, *op. cit.*, I, 29.

18. *Ibid.*, I, 229.

Among the many studies of Marvell, I wish to express a general appreciation of insights gained from the following: M. C. Bradbrook and M. G. L. Thomas, *Andrew Marvell*, Cambridge University Press, 1940; Frank Kermode, "The Argument of Marvell's 'Garden' ", *Essays in Criticism*, 2 (1952), pp. 225–41; Joseph Summers, "Marvell's 'Nature' ", *ELH*, 20 (1953), pp. 121–35; Don Cameron Allen, essays on "The Nymph Complaining" and "Upon Appleton House" in *Image and Meaning*, Baltimore, Johns Hopkins Press, 1960; John Edward Hardy, essay on "The Coronet" in *The Curious Frame*, Notre Dame, University of Notre Dame Press, 1962; Lawrence W. Hyman, *Andrew Marvell*, New York, Twayne, 1964; Harry Berger, Jr., "Marvell's 'Upon Appleton House': An Interpretation," *Southern Review* (Australia), I (1965), pp. 7–32; Pierre Legouis, *Andrew Marvell, Poet, Puritan, Patriot*, Oxford, Clarendon Press, 1965; Harold E. Toliver, *Marvell's Ironic Vision*, New Haven, Yale University Press, 1965; J. B. Leishman, *The Art of Marvell's Poetry*, London, Hutchinson, 1966; Stanley Stewart, *The Enclosed Garden*, Madison, University of Wisconsin Press, 1966.

Index

Index

term applied to Marvell, 154,
  156–8, 164, 169–70, 173–4,
  185, 190
term applied to Milton, 102
Mantua, Duke of, 174
Margoliouth, H. M., 202 (n 1)
Marino, Giambattista, 102
  La Galeria, 173
Martial, 64
Martin, L. C., 202
Marvell, Andrew, at Cam-
  bridge, 152; career of,
  compared with Crashaw's,
  152–3
collected poems, 159
contrasted with Crashaw,
  163–5
contrasted with Donne, 165–7
contrasted with Herbert,
  155–6
influenced by Carew, 154
influenced by Cavalier poets,
  153–4, 156, 162
influenced by Donne, 154,
  164–7
influenced by Herbert, 154–5
influenced by Jonson, 154,
  160, 164–5
Mannerist qualities, 154, 156–
  8, 164, 169–70, 173–4, 185,
  190
pastoral tradition, use of, 154,
  156–9, 175, 177, 182, 184–5,
  187
poems on Princess Anne, 152
political poems, 182, 187
portrait of, 150 (Fig. 30)
studies of, 204
wit, quality of, 186

Works:
  "Ametas and Thestylis
    making Hay-Ropes,"
    158–9
  "Bermudas," 175–7
  "Clorinda and Damon,"
    156–8
  "The Coronet," 154–5
  "Damon the Mower," 177–
    8
  "The Definition of Love,"
    165–7
  "A Dialogue between the
    Resolved Soul, and
    Created Pleasure," 158–
    60
  "A Dialogue between the
    Soul and Body," 160–1
  "A Dialogue between
    Thyrsis and Dorinda,"
    158
  "On a Drop of Dew," 161–3
  "Eyes and Tears," 163–5
  "The Fair Singer," 154
  "The Gallery," 173–5, 203
    (n 8)
  "The Garden," 171–3
  "To his Coy Mistress,"
    154, 161, 167–9
  "To his Noble Friend Mr.
    Richard Lovelace," 153
  "An Horatian Ode," 152–
    3, 171
  "The Match," 154
  "The Mower against Gar-
    dens," 178–9
  "The Mower to the Glo-
    Worms," 177
  "The Mower's Song," 177